The Gifts
of the
Holy Spirit

by

Dr. Rodney M. Howard-Browne

Unless otherwise indicated, all scriptural quotations are from the King James Version of the Bible. Scriptures marked NKJ are from the New King James Version. Emphasis within Scripture is the author's own.

The Gifts of the Holy Spirit
ISBN 978-1-63443-609-0

Copyright © 2000 by
Rodney M. Howard-Browne

Published by
Revival Ministries International
P.O. Box 292888
Tampa, FL 33687 U.S.A.
www.revival.com
1 (813) 971-9999

Printed in the United States of America.

All rights reserved under International Copyright Law.
Contents and/or cover may not be reproduced in whole or in part in any form without the express written consent of the publisher.

Dedication

To all those who have gone before us, whom God has used in a wonderful way because they offered themselves to Him and said, "Lord, use me."

To the new breed of men and women, who will yield themselves to the Lord so He can flow through them in a mighty way to touch the lives and meet the needs of a hurting humanity.

Contents

Contents

Foreword

I felt led of the Lord to put into a book on the gifts of the Holy Spirit some practical aspects of the gifts, how to cooperate and flow with the Spirit of God, and how to yield to Him to be a vessel that He can use.

God is not looking for perfect people, just yielded vessels through whom He can flow to touch the lives of hurting humanity. God uses us in spite of us, not because of us—but because of Jesus and because we offer ourselves to Him and say, "Lord, use me."

In a day and age when the occult, psychics, and cults are on the rise, may the Church rise up and let the ministry of Jesus be seen in the earth again through His Body. I pray that as you read this book you will be stirred in your spirit to contend for the gifts. You will never know when you might need them.

Dr. Rodney M. Howard-Browne Th.D, D.Min, D.D.

June 2000

Part One

Laying the Foundation

Chapter 1

Concerning Spiritual Gifts

The first thing we need to know about the nine gifts of the Holy Spirit is that all of them are supernatural gifts. None of them is a natural gift. You cannot acquire any of them by going to a school and learning them, nor can you explain them as a natural talent you may possess.

In other words, the gifts of the Holy Spirit don't come from you; they come from Heaven. You are the *vessel* through which these gifts flow.

In the natural, you could compare the process to what a reflector does on the back of an automobile. In itself, that reflector has nothing but a bright light shining into it, which reflects out of it; and the reflected light is at the same intensity as the light that's reflected into it.

It almost looks as if the reflector has a bright light inside it, but it doesn't. The bright light shines into it, and then the light is reflected out of the reflector.

It's the same with the gifts of the Spirit. You and I are only *reflectors* of the glory of God. God shines His glory into us, and then it flows out through us. He begins to move, but the gifts aren't ours; they're God's. God just uses us as His vessel. It's important for us to bear in mind that we're only the vessel, because some people start claiming the gifts as their own, and they eventually think they're really something.

Did you know that gifts are not a sign of being spiritual? I've known some people who prophesied and spoke in tongues, but they were the most carnal Christians in the whole church! Yes, Sister Bucketmouth may get up and speak in tongues, and Brother Doodad may interpret it, but they may be the very ones who are causing trouble all the time.

When you operate in the gifts you are yielding to the Holy Spirit. If you are not living a holy life, you will yield to a wrong spirit and be used of the devil, just like Samson. One minute he was in the Spirit; the next he was in the flesh; and the conflict was destructive. (See Judges 13–16.)

The motive when it comes to the operation of the gifts is so important...it must be the love of God. Read First Corinthians 13—the whole chapter. Love must be the motivation out of a pure heart that is consecrated to the Lordship of Jesus Christ. Remember that it is the Holy Spirit—therefore, get rid of sin and be holy. Then you will be a vessel that God can continually use.

Reminder: God Still Uses Donkeys

People have assumed that the gifts are a sign of maturity, but God uses whom He chooses—and God will use a donkey. He used a donkey in the Old Testament, and He still uses donkeys today!

It excited me when I read that God used that prophet's donkey, because that meant if God could use a donkey, He can use me. And if God can use me, He can surely use you.

So the gifts of the Holy Spirit are not ours; they belong to God. We don't own them. You can't say, as some do, "I have the gift of healing(s)." No, you don't. God uses you in that area, but you really don't *have* this gift. If you did, you could move in it when you wanted to, and you can't.

That's one of the biggest errors people make. They think, *I can do what I want to*, so they step out and start to operate on their own. If you step out without the power of God, and you step out into an area for which there's no anointing, you are opening the door for familiar spirits to come and operate!

We don't own the gifts. They belong to God. They belong to His Spirit. All we do is flow *with* the Spirit, and He flows *through* us. We yield our body, which is the temple of the Holy Spirit, to Him.

Obviously, the Holy Spirit cannot speak or prophesy without our vocal chords, so we yield our members to Him. By yielding ourselves to the Spirit of God, He flows through us—but it's always God. It's never to be you.

If someone tells you, "Oh, brother, that was a wonderful prophecy," you can't accept his compliment, because you really did nothing but open your mouth. The prophecy was from the Spirit of God who flowed through you.

If we get this issue of the "ownership" of the gifts settled now, once and for all, we'll understand that God can use anyone. In fact, God will use a five-year-old child if that five-year-old child will let Him!

Edification, Exhortation, and Comfort?

The Bible says that the gifts of the Spirit are given to us for edification, exhortation, and comfort. God never placed the gifts of the Spirit in the Church to pull the Church down. So if someone gets up and prophesies, "Yea, saith the Lord, thou shalt all die by eight o'clock in the morning, for I have no more need of thee, thou ugly outfits," we know that wasn't God.

How do we know it? First, did it edify us? No. It didn't edify us. Did it exhort us? How many were exhorted? Did it comfort us, telling us we were going to die tomorrow morning at eight o'clock? Hardly.

Yet some people go around spreading gloom and doom wherever they go. Here's an example: "God told me He's going to *get* you! You've come against Him, and that's it! God is drawing a line. He's going to get you!" No, that's not God. That's not edification, exhortation, and comfort. That's another spirit.

The gifts of the Spirit will always work when someone is in dire straits or in need, and we will discuss this further in another chapter, when we study the utterance gifts.

Too many Christians are going around desiring a word from the Lord. "Give me a word! I want a word," they say. One such person telephoned a great prophet of God at four o'clock one morning and asked, "Brother, do you have a *word* for me?"

"Yes," he replied. "Go back to bed!"

Because everyone wants a word, people start prophesying over each other. "Yea, the Lord shall say, thou shalt not come as thou hast gone, and thou shalt not look to the left and up and down and sideways and this way and that way..." and by the end of it, you don't know what they said.

God often moves supernaturally when people are in dire straits or in need, to help them. So don't go around looking for a word, because if you *do* get one, it could be a sign that hard times are coming!

Every time I get a prophecy from someone, I say, "Oh, no! This means I've got to stand on this word. I'm entering a fight, and God is giving me the encouragement I need to see it through."

Remember, Paul told Timothy, "...according to the prophecies which went before on thee, that thou by them mightest war a good warfare" (1 Tim. 1:18).

It's by the gifts of utterance that God comes to comfort you in your time of need. He lifts you up, builds you up, and says, "The situation you are going through is dark. It looks like you'll never make it through, but don't worry: I made a way for you, and I'm going to raise you up." Then you shall know that you can cling to the Word of the Lord through the dark periods of your life.

No Word Is a Good Word

So don't go around looking for a word and begging, "Oh, brother, give me a word." If you don't have a word, go to *the Word*, and rejoice in it.

I like what one preacher said about it: "I go as much by what God *doesn't* say about something as by what He *does* say." If God has told you to do something, you've been doing it for a year, and God hasn't said anything else, obviously He's happy with you, and He wants you to keep on doing it. Just keep flowing with God. Don't keep looking for a word.

One minister came to me and said, "Let's get in the car and go see this woman of God. She's a prophetess. She'll give us a word!"

I said, "I'm not going."

"What do you mean you're not going? The Bible says, 'Despise not prophesying.'"

I replied, "Brother, listen. I don't despise prophesying, and if that woman has a word for me, she can come here and give it to me. But I'm not going to go to her house only to find that I arrived on an 'off' day for her, with the result that she prophesies me *out* of the will of God.

"I *know* what God has told me to do. Besides that, I've got other people around me who are quite capable of giving me a word, if God wants them to. I don't need to drive five hundred miles to get some prophetess to prophesy over me."

Edification, exhortation, and comfort—that's why all nine gifts are in the Church.

Diversities and Differences

If you look at our text, First Corinthians 12:4, you will see that the Bible says there are "...*diversities* of gifts, but the same Spirit."

Then look at verse 5, and you'll find that there are "...*differences* of administrations, but the same Lord."

The next verse tells us there are "...*diversities* of operations, but it is the same God which worketh all in all."

So we've seen diversities of gifts, differences of administrations, and diversities of operations by the same Spirit, the same Lord, the same God.

What does that tell us? It tells us that *God does not move the same way all the time.* It means that God is a unique God. God made every one of you unique, and when the Spirit of God flows through you, the gift comes through with *your* personality behind it.

If you're a quiet person, you're not going to scream and shout. God is going to use you *as you are*, with your personality, your nature, and your character. But God wants you to be the best you can be.

I can only be myself; I can't be anyone else. And you can only be yourself. I'll be me and you'll be you. I'll be the best me, and you'll be the best you. But I can't be you, and you can't be me. If we'll just be ourselves, we'll have a good time in the things of God.

Oracles, Not Echoes

God wants to use you, and when He does, it will be different. Some people attend our meetings and say, "It's different." Yes, it is different. God wants to be different.

God once told me, "There are so many echoes in the world, but I'm going to raise up a voice in this last generation that will not echo the others. They will speak as a voice, as an oracle of God."

They will be different, but it will be the same Spirit. It will be the same Lord. It will be the same God which worketh all in all.

Don't criticize something just because it doesn't work the way you think it should. Some critics in ancient Palestine once said, "I don't know about that guy...He spits on the ground and puts clay on people's eyes."

Jesus was different, wasn't He? Think about it—Jesus spat on the ground, made clay, put the clay on the blind man's eyes, and instructed him, "Go wash."

The Spitting Preacher

How many of you would like to go to the First Church of the Spitting Preacher? If that happened today, people would complain, "I was clean until that spitting preacher spat on the ground and made me dirty. Then He told me to go wash. I'm never going back to *that* church again!"

It's one thing to read it in the Bible, but it's another thing to see it happen before your eyes! Do you agree that spitting on the ground, making clay, and putting it on a man's eyes is different? Jesus, then, was different.

In fact, if Jesus were here today, He'd be kicked out of most churches. They wouldn't have Him! They'd run Him out of town, and they'd want to throw Him over a cliff, just like the people of Nazareth did in Bible days.

We want to go to church, sing a few songs, and then go home again. And if anything a little bit out of the ordinary happens, we get very upset about it. "Well! I don't know if *that's* God," we're quick to complain.

First of all, ask yourself the question, "Is it edifying? Is it exhorting and comforting?"

If I prayed for ten people and all of them ran out and shot themselves, you could conclude, "Something's wrong here!" But if they're all blessed, healed, set free, delivered, and wanting to serve God, you know it must be God. A child of three can see that.

Verse 7 of our text is very important: "But the manifestation of the Spirit is given to every man to profit withal." The nine gifts are for our profit, or help. In other words, if you don't have the nine gifts of the Spirit not only in your church, but also in your private life, you are running at a loss.

Inside Information

We once received negative reports about getting back to the United States because there were problems with our papers. I remember visiting the travel agent at that time. She said, "It's going to be very difficult for you to get back into the States."

I smiled at her and said, "Book the tickets." Then I started laughing.

I said, "Do you know why I'm laughing? I've got *inside information!*"

How did I know we would be allowed into the States? God spoke to me through the word of knowledge, and then He gave me a word of wisdom, telling me exactly what to do. We got right in, we came right out, and were going right back.

A preacher friend was sitting in a chair nearby. When the agent asked, "How are you going to get in?" and I replied, "I've got *inside information*," the power of God hit him, and he started laughing uncontrollably. He got drunk in the Spirit, and he nearly fell out on the floor of the travel agency!

We had a whale of a time! Why? Because I had inside information. It's easy when you've got inside information. You know more about what's going on.

Let me tell you, *we are not subject to the knowledge that we can receive with our five senses, because we can tap into God's knowledge.* We can tap into God! We can find out what He has to say about our situation.

It's like you're caught in rush-hour traffic on your way home. You're in the middle of a traffic jam, and you can't see a way out. Then you turn on your radio and hear a traffic report from the helicopter pilot overhead. He says, "Turn down Main Street, get on 52nd Street, and you'll be on the highway and escape the traffic jam." You follow his advice, and you're out of the traffic jam in five minutes—because he sees more than you do.

> We are not subject to the knowledge that we can receive with our five senses, because we can tap into God's knowledge.

Sometimes in life we're caught in the middle of a mess, and we can't find our way out. But there is One above who sees and knows all. If we will look to Him, He will show us the way out, and we will escape, rejoicing!

Chapter 2

Operating in the Gifts of the Spirit

There are three categories of the gifts of the Holy Spirit:

1. Three of them *say* something (Gifts of *Utterance*)
2. Three of them *do* something (Gifts of *Power*)
3. Three of them *reveal* something (Gifts of *Revelation*)

What you find, as you study the operations of these gifts, is that *they often overlap.* For example, a word of prophecy may come forth, but it's not really pure prophecy; it's a word of knowledge linked with a word of wisdom, and it comes forth to bless a person.

Sometimes there will be two or three different gifts in operation at one time. That's what happens with the working of miracles. It takes the gift of faith to have the working of miracles. They work together hand in glove.

When you find someone who yields to the Holy Spirit concerning the gift of faith, they will have miracles, like

Brother Smith Wigglesworth had. This bold man raised about 20 people from the dead!

If you have the gift of faith, however, you'll scare people. You'll frighten people. You'll make religious people *nervous.*

Wigglesworth and the Gift of Faith

They called Brother Wigglesworth one day and said, "Brother Wigglesworth, would you come to the house and pray for Uncle Fred? He's dying." He said, "I'll come just now."

They called him again and said, "Please, you've got to come! He's in a bad way. He's dying!"

He said, "I told you, I'll come in a little while."

They called him back a few minutes later and said, "Don't bother. Uncle Fred is dead."

He said, "I'm coming."

When Wigglesworth arrived, he found Uncle Fred dead and already in his coffin. There were about 60 mourners in the room. Wigglesworth walked right up to the coffin, yanked the corpse out of it, pushed the body up against the wall, and said, "Walk, in Jesus' name!" The corpse fell to the floor.

Wigglesworth just bent down, picked it up, and stood it against the wall again. He commanded, "Walk, in the name of Jesus!" The corpse fell to the floor again.

If I had been with him, that's about the time I'd have said, "Excuse me, Brother Wigglesworth. I have an appointment I need to keep elsewhere. I'll see you next month."

But Wigglesworth didn't stop. You see, *when the gift of faith comes on you, you don't take no for an answer!* He bent down, picked the corpse up again, slammed it against the wall, and thundered, "I told you to walk!" And the man walked!

Wigglesworth turned and calmly walked out the door. It didn't bother him. Why? Because it was not his faith; it was the gift of faith.

The Key to Operating the Gifts

We need to bear in mind that the gifts are divided as the Holy Spirit wills, not as we will. *This is the biggest key to operating in the gifts of the Spirit: It's as He wills.*

All we need to do is make ourselves available to be a vessel through which God's power can flow in the form of the nine manifestations, or gifts, of the Holy Spirit.

Ask God to use you as such a vessel. Ask Him to use you—then start expecting the gifts to come into manifestation in your life.

When I preach on this subject, the power of God usually starts to fall on people as I speak, without my doing anything. They begin to get blessed and healed out in the congregation without anyone laying hands on them.

> We need
> to bear
> in mind that
> the gifts
> are divided
> as the
> Holy Spirit wills,
> not as we will.

The Role of Faith

Is it by faith alone that the gifts of the Spirit operate?
That's probably one of the most frequently asked questions about the gifts.

Some say, "Well, you just operate by faith." One man, however, came to me and said, "I don't even wait on the anointing anymore; I just prophesy."

I said, "That figures, judging from the junk that's been coming out of your mouth for the last six weeks."

People think that you simply string words together, and the more Elizabethan it sounds, the better. There's nothing wrong with prophesying with thous and thees—I do it—but just because you've got the thous, the thees, the yeas, and the nays in your prophecy doesn't guarantee it is genuine. We may need to take the yeas out so we can get to what the Spirit of God is actually trying to say!

God is limited to the proportion or measure that you yield yourself to His flow through you. So *it is not by faith alone that the gifts of the Spirit operate.* There are two more important elements involved in the operation of the nine gifts—love and anointing.

The Role of Love

First, *faith* is a major element in operating in the gifts of the Spirit, but it is not the only element.

Second, it is by *love* that the gifts operate. You can prophesy and operate in all the other gifts, but the Bible says in First Corinthians 13:1 that if you don't have any love, you're like "sounding brass, or a tinkling cymbal."

Some people are like a noisy gong. You'll frequently find them in church: There's Brother Gong, Sister Gong, and all the little Gongs. They've got no love. They'll get up in every service and do their thing, regardless of what else is happening.

When I was growing up in a Pentecostal church, we had such a woman in our congregation. She'd get up in every service—it didn't matter when—and speak in tongues. When sinners sat near this woman, Sister Racundu, they'd almost take off when she suddenly burst forth with tongues in the middle of a sermon.

My brother and I used to watch her. We could tell when she was going to speak out. We called her Sister Racundu after the word she most often used. We also had a brother who would go, "Ra-ba-ba-banda," so naturally we called him Brother Rabababanda.

The Gifts Come on Wings of Love

So the operation of the gifts is not only by faith—any donkey can bray. It's by love—the love of God—that the gifts will operate.

Loving people and desiring to see them healed, blessed, touched, and reached by the love of God cause the gifts to operate. The more you love people, the stronger the gifts will begin to operate.

Love is the wings on which the gifts flow.

Someday, without your even realizing it, the gifts will simply start working in your life. You'll be talking to someone, and you'll think you're just having a conversation with him. Meanwhile, you'll be actually prophesying to him! You'll be telling him facts about his life. He'll sit there and his eyes will get as big as saucers as he listens to you. I'm telling you, the power of God will start to fall on you when you love people.

The Role of the Anointing

Third, the operation of the gifts of the Spirit works by *the anointing*. To review, it works by faith, love, and the anointing.

This is where many people have a problem. They know something about faith. They know a little about love. But they don't know anything about the anointing.

The anointing is that awesome presence of God that will come and begin to touch people.

In some of our services, the anointing falls on people like a sensation of heat. They get healed in their bodies right there in their seat. People have come to me afterwards and said, "I had cancer, and I felt a heat go right through my body." What was that heat? It was the anointing.

But some people wouldn't know the anointing if it slapped them on the ear!

They think the anointing is a nice suit.

They think the anointing is a big car.

They think the anointing is a fine house.

They think the anointing is how eloquently a person speaks.

No, the anointing is the presence of God—and the anointing touches people's hearts.

That's what happens when the gift of healing(s) begins to manifest: People start getting healed all over the congregation. That's what used to happen in Kathryn Kuhlman's meetings.

People came by the busloads, and before they even got to the building, some were throwing away their crutches. People passing the building would jump out of their wheelchairs. As Miss Kuhlman walked through airports, it is said that people began falling out under the power of God!

This is real. It's the presence and the anointing of God. The Church is looking for it, and the world is looking for it, too, whether they know it or not.

The Scripture First John 2:20 says, "But ye have an unction from the Holy One, and ye know all things." *You can't function without an unction!* You must wait for that unction, that anointing—especially with the vocal gifts.

Stay With the Anointing

I wait for the unction all the time; I wait for the burning of the Spirit of God within. That burning, that churning, bubbles like a boiling pot inside, because that's what the word *prophesy* means.

To prophesy means, "to bubble forth, to tumble forth, and to spring forth." I wait for the anointing to come; but once it lifts, I stop. Some people go with the anointing for 30 seconds and continue for another five minutes without the anointing. *Stay with the anointing!* Don't go beyond it.

The Scripture First John 2:27 says, "But the anointing which ye have received of Him abideth in you, and ye need not that any man teach you: but as the same anointing teacheth you of all things, and is truth, and is no lie, and even as it hath taught you, ye shall abide in Him."

This is the truth, and it's a comfort to know that the Holy Spirit will teach you as you abide in Him, and as you walk and live in the anointing.

How does the anointing teach you? You will walk into a store, the anointing will fall on you, and you'll ask, "What do You want me to do, God?" You'll be talking to someone, the anointing will fall on you, and you'll say, "Lord, what do You want me to do?"

Mental vs. Spiritual

*A*lways be sensitive to the Spirit of God. Don't try to work the gifts with your head. The gifts don't operate in the mental realm; they operate in the spiritual realm.

Furthermore, you must stir yourself up for the gifts to begin to operate. You can't be half dead and expect God to move through you! The Bible says, "David encouraged himself in the Lord his God" (1 Sam. 30:6b). You, too, need to build yourself up, or edify yourself. Jude 20 says, "But ye, beloved, building up yourselves on your most holy faith, praying in the Holy Ghost."

The more *edified* you are, the more you can edify others. The more *exhorted* you are, the more you can exhort others. The more *comforted* you are, the more you can comfort others. The more joyful you are, the more you can bring to others.

If you're sad, down, and distraught, you will take that with you wherever you go. But if you're full of the Spirit of God, the anointing of God will flow forth from you. It will just happen. You can't make it happen. You can't say, "I must now prophesy. I must now move in the gifts." It will happen automatically. God will begin to move.

Walking in the supernatural must become a way of life to you.

Hungry and Thirsty for God

I was raised in a Pentecostal church. We'd go to church every Sunday morning, Sunday night, Wednesday night, and Friday night. Saturday night was Cottage Prayer Meeting in our home. We went to church every time the doors were opened!

That's a major problem with believers today: They don't come to church every time the doors open. Some members come once a week on Sunday. Some come once every two weeks. Others come once every three weeks.

You need to be in church every time the doors open, especially in these last days. The Bible says, "Not forsaking the assembling of ourselves together, as the manner of some is; but exhorting one another: and so much the more, as ye see the day approaching" (Heb. 10:25).

In 1979, I got hungry and thirsty for God to move in my life. I said, "God, I want your power. I want your power!"— and it happened. The power of God fell on me for four days. I wasn't the same person afterwards.

Then, in 1980, the first year I was in the ministry, I began to learn more about flowing with the anointing. I learned that sometimes you'll feel a prompting, or an urge, that comes like a desire. There will be a strong leading to begin to step out and flow in the gifts.

Learning to Be Obedient

Once I was conducting a service and I noticed a well-dressed man on the front row. He looked like a millionaire! The Spirit of God said to me, "Tell him that even though he's in dire straits financially, I'm going to give him a miracle."

I said, "God, I can't call that man up here and tell him that. He's a millionaire—just look at him. I can't tell *him* he's in dire straits. Everyone will think I'm nuts."

The Lord said, "Call him and tell him that even though he's in dire straits financially, I'm going to give him a miracle."

I said, "I'm not going to do it. He looks like Donald Trump!"

But I obeyed God and called the man forward. I gave him the word of the Lord, and to my astonishment, he started to cry—because, as it turned out, he needed half a million dollars by the next morning!

It doesn't matter how you are dressed; if you need half a million dollars by the next morning, you're in dire straits financially in anyone's language! I didn't know it by looking at the man, but God did.

Learn to flow in the gifts by *doing*. Don't be afraid to make mistakes. Everyone is so afraid of missing it! It will be easy for you once you know the anointing and presence of God, once you know the Holy Spirit, once you know how to build yourself up in the Holy Spirit, and once you learn how to yield yourself to the Spirit.

It's easy, because all you need to do is instantly obey when the Spirit of God speaks to you. Sometimes this comes in gentle promptings or leadings. They come so softly, you may miss them if you're not sensitive to the Holy Spirit. Some of the most important things in my life have come so quietly and softly that I could have missed them.

Follow the Love of God

God sometimes speaks in a seemingly audible voice. And sometimes He speaks through that still, small voice deep inside of you. Whichever way He speaks to you, follow the prompting, the leading, the anointing, and the love of God.

For example, I may walk into a church and the love of God will reach out toward certain people. I'll be deeply moved with compassion in my heart toward them. Then God will give me a word and say, "Now call that man out. Tell him this and that."

I will call the man forward, and as I begin to tell him these things by the Spirit of God, the anointing will come on him, he'll start weeping, and the power of God will set him free then and there.

So learn to obey God's voice instantly. Act on it. Jesus said, "I don't do anything unless I first see My Father do it" (see Jn. 5:19). That statement contains an important key:

Don't *say* anything until the Holy Spirit says it first.

Don't *do* anything until you see Him do it first.

And don't *reveal* anything until He reveals it first.

Don't Launch Out Only on Hope

If followed, these safeguards will keep unwise and overly zealous people from jumping up and *hoping* they have a word for someone.

— 20 —

"Someone here has a pain in their wrist." No one gets up.

"The pain just moved to the elbow." Again, no one responds.

"It moved down to the lower back." Nothing. They go on and on, naming various aches and pains until they eventually find someone in the building who has a pain in his big toe.

"Come here, brother. I knew it was you all the time!"

With such safeguards in mind, you needn't be so afraid of missing it. Actually, God's not concerned whether you miss it or not; God's major concern is if you *repent* when you do miss it. Just tell the people it affected, "I'm sorry. Look, I felt God was telling me that, and obviously I missed it. I ate too much pizza last night."

And then repent and ask God to forgive you and go on.

You missed it in the past as you were learning the ways of the Spirit, and you'll miss it in the future as you continue to learn the ways of the Spirit. In fact, you will miss it at times from now until Jesus comes. Why? Because you're human!

I suggest you make the following confession:

Confession

I'm not afraid to miss it. I'm not afraid to step out of the boat and walk on the water of the supernatural.

I'd rather be a wet water walker than a dry boat sitter. I'm going to walk on the water of the things of the Spirit of God. I'm going to walk in the supernatural.

I'm going to stir myself up in the Holy Spirit. I'm going to stir myself up in the anointing. I'm going to stir myself up to move in the supernatural.

I'm hungry for the nine gifts! I covet earnestly the best gifts, for they're the ones I need at the time.

Put into practice the things you have learned in this chapter. Stir yourself up to walk in the supernatural. Tomorrow when you wake up, pray the following:

Prayer

God, today I tune myself into the wavelength of the Spirit of God. I've got an ear, and the Bible says, "My sheep know My voice, and the voice of a stranger they will not follow" (see Jn. 10:4-5).

I listen to the voice of the Spirit of God, and I yield myself to the Spirit of God, that He may flow through me.

And, Lord, You lead me to the people. You speak to me. I will obey. I, Your sheep, will obey and do what You tell me to do.

If you do these things, you'll begin to see God move through you. Your life will become an exciting adventure!

Part Two

The Gifts of Utterance

Chapter 3

God Speaks to the Church

The gifts of utterance say something. Through these gifts, God speaks to the Church. Through these gifts, God speaks for edification, exhortation, and comfort to the Body of Christ.

The three utterance gifts are:

1.   Prophecy
2.   Divers (diverse) kinds of tongues
3.   Interpretation of tongues

As we study these three utterance gifts, we realize that each of them is supernatural (as are all nine gifts of the Spirit). You can't get up one day and decide, "Well, I think I'll prophesy." You'd better keep your mouth closed. You can't get up and think, "Well, I think I'll give you a message in tongues." Keep the message to yourself. You can't get up and say, "Well, I think I'll interpret that."

You either have the anointing for it, or you don't. If you do, the word of the Lord will come to you, and it will burn deep down in your belly. And as you open your mouth to speak, there will be an unction, or anointing, with it. It will flow forth like a river, and it will bring life to every place it falls.

The gifts of the Spirit always bring life and allow the presence of God to be made manifest. They always leave you feeling edified, exhorted, and comforted.

No one should come to you and say, "Thus saith the Lord, thou shalt die by tomorrow morning," and not give you a way out of such a dire prediction. There are many prophets of doom. And if some people don't like you, they will prophesy against you! You might even say that such a thing borders on "Christian witchcraft."

The Gift of Prophecy

Let's begin by looking at the supernatural gift of prophecy. What is the definition of prophecy? _Prophecy is a supernatural utterance in a known tongue._

In other words, it's a tongue that's known to you. If your known language is Chinese, it will come forth in Chinese. If it is English, it will come forth in English.

Prophecy is an inspired utterance. Prophecy is not something you make up. Prophecy comes by the Spirit of God. It comes out of your belly. It's given by God for your benefit.

The word _prophesy_ means "to flow forth, to bubble forth, to tumble forth, and to spring forth."

This supernatural utterance in a known tongue will edify, exhort, and comfort you. These are the guidelines for prophecy.

One of the things I think we need to realize about prophecy is that it is _conditional._ People have frequently come to me and asked, "Why is it that someone prophesied to me, 'Thus saith the Lord, I'll do this and that and the other'—and it never came to pass?" Because prophecy is *conditional*.

If God has a plan for your life, and someone prophesies His plan and purpose to you, but you run from it, it will never come to pass. In that case, the problem is not with God; the problem is with you. Remember this: The problem is never with God.

So if someone prophesies something to you that you know is the truth, but you run from it because you don't want to do the will of God for your life, don't complain when it doesn't come to pass.

Willing *and* Obedient

The Bible says, "If ye be *willing* and *obedient*, ye shall eat the good of the land" (Is. 1:19). Many people are willing, but they're not obedient. Many are obedient, but they're not willing.

They're like the little boy who was standing up on the seat, and his father said, "Son, sit down." The little boy replied, "I don't want to!" His dad said, "Son, I said to sit down." He said, "No!" And his dad jerked him down into the seat.

He looked up at his dad and said, "Daddy, I'm sitting down on the *outside*, but I'm standing up on the *inside!*"

And that's how a lot of Christians are: They're sitting down on the outside, pretending to be obedient; but they're standing up on the inside, harboring rebellion in their heart. The Scripture says we must be both willing *and* obedient in order to eat the good of the land.

Prophecy can be abused, as can all the gifts of the Spirit.

Preparing to Prophesy

U sually, God is not going to send an angel to earth to prophesy. Most of the time, He's going to use the Body of Christ as we yield to Him.

You may wonder, "How can I become available to be used for these utterance gifts?" Pray every day, "God, if You want me to speak, give me the word and I'll speak." And then make yourself available.

It might be a prompting, a leading, a pulling, a drawing of the Spirit of God to someone because you love them and want to help them. God may give you a word for them, saying, "Tell them, 'Thus says the Lord...' "

As I pointed out in an earlier chapter, you will surely make mistakes on your way to maturity in the things of God, but when you do, simply repent and keep doing the best you can. You may start with only a few words, a line, or a sentence, but as you learn to yield more and more to the Spirit of God, you will grow, and God will use you more and more strongly in that area.

When a person has the gift of prophecy operating in his or her ministry, it's not because God gives it especially to them; it's because they yield to God constantly in that area. They're listening to what God wants to say, because God wants to bless His people.

Despise Not Prophesying

B ecause prophecy is often abused, prophecy is often despised. I see prophecy coming forth in local churches, and the people sit there unmoved. It's obvious that they're judging the prophecy—which is scriptural. The Bible *says* to judge prophecy. But you should know by the first two words if it's God or not. And it's never going to be one hundred percent perfect, because the vessel that is yielding to the Spirit of God is not one hundred percent perfect.

Listen to the overall picture that the Spirit of God is painting, and receive it for yourself. Don't sit there and criticize a little flaw, such as, "Oh, he put a 'yea' in the wrong place, so that can't be God."

Receive what God is saying. Don't despise prophesying. It's for your benefit. It's for your edification. It's for your exhortation. It's for comfort for the Body of Christ.

One area of prophecy that is frequently abused is the area of guidance. People are always wanting a word. I know people who collect prophecies. They've got books full of prophecies, and much of it is a bunch of ye, yea, and hitherto that doesn't mean anything!

If you are running around looking for *guidance* from prophecy, you will be misled. The Bible does not say, "For as many as are led by the prophets, they are the sons of God." It says, "For as many as are led by the Spirit of God, they are the sons of God" (Rom. 8:14).

Prophecy Only Confirms

Prophecy must never *guide* you. Prophecy must *confirm* what you already know in your heart.

> Prophecy must never *guide* you. Prophecy must *confirm* what you already know in your heart.

If I come to you and say, "Yea, saith the Lord, thou art called to the land of China. Thou shalt leave within three months," and you don't even know how to hold chopsticks, you're in *big* trouble!

But let's say that you've had China, China, China on your heart for ten years and I, a perfect stranger, walk up to you and say, "God says that He's going to take you to China." Suddenly this word goes off inside you like a bomb, and you say, "My, my, he could never have known that! That *has* to be God, because I've been wanting to go for years, and this is confirmation to me that God wants me to go." Wouldn't that bless you?

So if someone comes to you and prophesies that you are going to China, but you don't know anything about it, don't go. Stay at home and wait for confirmation. Wait for God's plan. Prophecy must be *confirmation*, not revelation and information.

If you asked someone, "Why did you marry that person?" and they replied, "Well, Brother Doodad prophesied I was to marry that person," the problem is, Brother Doodad's not married to that person—you are!

"Why did you get that job?"

"Well, So-and-so prophesied to me that I must get that job."

The problem is, So-and-so is not collecting the paycheck every month—you are!

Follow your heart. Follow your spirit. Don't be misled. Follow peace. Let peace be the umpire and reign in your heart.

Misguided "Prophets"

I have prophecies given to me all the time, and I know immediately if they're of God or not. Recently, a brother gave me a word from the Lord, and it was confirmation of what God was saying to me. He had tears in his eyes as he gave me the word.

I told him, "Yes, that's what I've been praying about and believing God for. That's confirmation to me of what God is saying to me."

However, not all the words given to me are actually from the Lord. Some people try to prophesy me to their church. They say, "The Lord would say that thou shalt come to this church and thou shalt stay here." My reply to one woman was, "Sister, when God tells me that, then I'll do something about it."

A family began following me from meeting to meeting in a western state. They'd show up on the front row in every service. They wanted to see me, so I took them out for a meal.

The man told me, "God told me I'm going to join your ministry—starting *tonight!*"

I said, "Is that right?"

He replied, "Brother, as my soul liveth, I shall not leave thee!"

And I thought to myself, "Brother, as thy soul liveth, thou *shalt* leave me, for if thou dost not leave me, thy soul shalt not live anymore!"

Then the man had the audacity to follow me to my hotel and try to find my room. I had to confront him and say, "Brother, I can think of five hundred other people who will join my ministry before you do.

"First of all," I said, "I don't know you from a bar of soap! Second..."

He interrupted me. He said, "Brother, you *need* me! I was in the service tonight and I picked up a lot of things in the Spirit that you don't know about!"

The problem was, if this man was as spiritual as he claimed to be, he would have been used of God in his own meetings, and he would not have had to follow someone else, to tell him how to do it.

He got mad at me for not hiring him on the spot. He asked, "Which town are you going to from here?"

I said, "Brother, if God's told you you're going to travel with me, then I guess when I get to the next town, you're going to be right there sitting on the front row. I'm not telling you anything." We haven't seen him since, but if he shows up, I'm going to tell him to go home.

You wouldn't believe some of the so-called prophecies we've heard from well-meaning, sincere, good people. Even though prophecy can be abused, don't throw the baby out with the bath water, so to speak. To put it another way, eat the meat (the good part) and leave the bones (the bad).

Counterfeit Prophecies

Some of these counterfeit prophecies can be *hilarious.* One person got up and said, "The Lord would say unto thee, fear has come upon the land, such fear as never before, so that even I, the Lord your God, am afraid." Can you picture God sitting on His throne with His knees knocking?

Around Christmastime, someone had a wonderful word from the Lord. He said, "And the Lord would wish thee all a merry Christmas." I thought, *I wonder if God sent down presents and Christmas cards, too.*

In the United States of America there is a beer by the name of Michelob. One Pentecostal lady, bless her darling heart, was so mad at the church she attended, she decided to get up and "prophesy" against them the next Sunday morning.

She got up and said, "The Lord would say, I've taken My Spirit out of this church. Yea, I've written 'Michelob' on the door." The word she should have used was "Ichabod," not "Michelob"! *Ichabod* means "the glory has departed." Can you imagine God putting a beer advertisement on the door of a church?

A man got up and prophesied at length about how "My servant Abraham led My people out of the land of Egypt." After ten minutes, he realized something was wrong, so he added, "The Lord would say unto thee, He's sorry He made a mistake. It wasn't Abraham; it was Moses."

We know that's not God! Not that the word of the Lord wasn't right, but we know it wasn't Abraham. The man should have admitted, "Folks, I missed it. The word of the Lord was right, because as God was with Moses, so He will be with you. But it wasn't Abraham; it was Moses."

A Bible school student got up one day and said, "The Lord would say unto thee, your praises are sweet before Me. Yea, saith the Lord, they're good for My health."

We can laugh at all these errors, but they don't take away from genuine prophecies. Those of you who worry so much about the flesh, the devil, and excesses will never see the real things of God.

I'm not going to worry about the flesh. I'm not going to worry about the devil. I'm not going to worry about the excesses. I want the real things of God, and I'm going to contend for them. I don't care how many flakes come along; I'm going through, and I'm going to see the real things of God.

And that goes for prophecy: I'm tired of all these wishy-washy prophecies. Surely God can say a bit more than what He is supposedly saying: "For the Lord would say, have a good day." Surely God's got more to say to this needy generation than "have a good day"!

Chapter 4

Prophecy: Inspired Utterance

Prophecy is inspired utterance bubbling forth out of your belly to bless other people. The Bible says, "For we know in part, and we prophesy in part" (1 Cor. 13:9).

We don't know *the whole*. We can only prophesy *the part*. If we knew the whole, we'd really be something, wouldn't we? Paul also says in this chapter, "For now we see through a glass, darkly..." (1 Cor. 13:12).

Romans 12:6 talks about prophesying "...according to the proportion of faith." You can only prophesy according to the measure of the faith that God has given you. That's why some people are used more in the area of prophecy: Their faith is greater in that area.

Step Out on the Water

To begin, you've got to step out on the water. The anointing will come; the unction will be there; the stirring will be in your heart. You've got to take the first step by opening your mouth as you do when you speak in tongues.

God isn't going to come and shake you until your teeth rattle and suddenly wonderful words of prophecy come out of your mouth. No, you will feel the stirring, and then you will yield yourself to the Spirit of God on the inside of you by opening your mouth, and you will begin to speak by the Spirit.

So when the anointing comes, flow with it. But when the anointing stops, stop! Don't prophesy for 20 seconds in the anointing and continue for 20 minutes in the flesh!

Prophecy will come forth in different forms. I know people who prophesy in rhyme, but that doesn't make *any* rhyme a prophecy. These people get up and say, "The Lord would say, you'll see My power in this hour in this land so grand. And you'll move and flow, and the truth you'll know and the victory you'll show."

There's nothing wrong with that, but just because something rhymes doesn't make it a prophecy. Maybe he's a poet and he doesn't know it!

There's a spirit to genuine prophecy. There's a *depth* to it. It's not just words coming out of your mouth. Prophecy is from the Spirit of God to the spirit of man. It's not coming from your head; it's coming from your heart. And you prophesy according to the proportion of your faith.

Wait for the Anointing!

The important thing about prophecy is to wait on the unction, or anointing.

And don't let people prophesy you out of your church, your job, or your marriage.

One man had 20 Scriptures that he believed directed him to divorce his wife. Also, many people had prophesied to him, "Yea, thou shalt get a divorce from that woman." The

Bible says that God *hates* divorce (see Mal. 2:16 NKJ), so how could that have been from God?

You can spend all your time on the negative and never get to the real, as that man did. Or, you can be so afraid that you're going to miss God that you never obey the voice of the Spirit.

I've found people who have been listening to a tape series on the love of God, and love has become such a revelation to them that when they open their mouth to prophesy, they prophesy about the love of God. It's inspired utterance concerning the love of God, and there's nothing wrong with it.

Be careful and make sure that when you *do* prophesy, it is under the anointing, and the anointing is there to back it up; that it is not just out of your human spirit, drawn from things that you have been studying and meditating upon.

It should come by the Spirit of God from Heaven and bubble out of your belly. You *know* it isn't you when it's genuine prophecy. You listen to it and think, "My, my my, that comes from God."

When the Anointing Falls

There have been times when I've been standing on the platform during praise and worship, and the gift of prophecy suddenly fell on me. I began to speak supernaturally. I became another person! In the Old Covenant, when Samuel anointed Saul, he prophesied that the Spirit of the Lord would come upon Saul, he would prophesy with a company of prophets, and he would be "turned into another man" (1 Sam. 10:6).

It's almost like I'm standing outside my body, hearing myself prophesy. But the prophecy is not coming from me; it's coming from Heaven above. My head is saying, "This is not me!" They're not my words; they're God's words.

People begin to shake and fall out under the power of God in their seats as the word of the Lord comes forth. No one touches them.

This has often happened to me, and I would like it to happen all the time, of course, but we have to flow with the anointing of the Spirit of God. Remember, prophecy is as *the Spirit* wills, not as we will.

You can't say, "I'm going to get up and prophesy now." However, you can prepare for the anointing to prophesy. You do this by stirring yourself up, by preparing your heart, and by waiting on the Spirit of God. Then, when the anointing comes, you flow with it. But you can only prophesy when the anointing comes!

The Anointing Clothes Us

If you get up to prophesy without the anointing, it's like someone getting up on the platform with no clothes on! That's because *the anointing is the clothing of the Spirit.*

As a matter of fact, it would be better to get up there with no clothes on than get up there *without* the anointing of God!

I don't want to give any word from the Lord or any prophecy without the anointing, because it's the equipment that's necessary to get the job done.

I wouldn't want to be caught dead without the anointing. When I die, I *still* want to have the anointing! I want to be like that Old Testament prophet, Elisha. According to Second Kings 13:20-21, there was so much anointing left in Elisha's *bones* that when a corpse was placed in his grave, the man was resurrected!

> I wouldn't want to be caught dead without the anointing. When I die, I *still* want to have the anointing!

How to Judge Prophecy

This is how to judge prophecy. When the word is coming forth, ask yourself these questions:

Does it glorify Jesus? If it does, it's God.

Does it line up with the Word? "Abraham leading My people out of the land of Egypt"—no. Moses—yes.

Does it produce liberty or bondage?

Does it uplift the congregation, or do they feel even worse after the so-called word of the Lord came forth? If it uplifts the people, you know it's God.

Some of you need to stir yourself up and get involved in the area of prophecy. But be open to correction. Don't come to church with some dingbat prophecy and get upset when someone corrects you. If you're big enough to open your mouth, you must be big enough to take correction.

Levels of Prophecy

There are different levels of prophecy. I want you to understand the difference between these two gifts: *the simple gift of prophecy and the deeper gift of prophecy* that accompanies the prophet's office.

Every believer can and should operate in the simple gift of prophecy. However, the simple gift of prophecy doesn't involve such matters as times, events, and places. That's getting into the deeper calling and operation of the gift of prophecy, linked to the prophet's office, which may also link up with the word of wisdom and the word of knowledge.

Remember, every one of these gifts will have a stronger anointing to it when it's linked to a fivefold ministry calling than when a lay person gives it.

For example, if a lay person got up and prophesied or if a pastor, prophet, or evangelist got up and prophesied, the anointing on the prophet would be greater than the anointing on the pastor, the evangelist, or the lay person.

Why is this? Because the lay person is stirring up the simple gift of prophecy. The pastor is moving in the pastoral office with the gift of prophecy, but the prophet is standing in the prophetic office, and the greatest anointing goes with that office.

How to Receive Prophecy

When some people get up and begin to speak, you can hear the word of the Lord coming forth, and you *know* it's not the simple gift of prophecy. There's a greater flow or anointing to it. It shouldn't take long to judge, yet some people I've met sit around for two weeks, wondering if it's God or not. Go ask God.

When I hear prophecy, I listen carefully to the first words coming out of his mouth; I don't look at the person delivering the word or how he's dressed. After all, God used Balaam's donkey to speak in the Old Testament (see Num. 22:28), and He still uses donkeys today.

What I want to hear are *the words* the person is speaking. And I don't listen from my head; I listen from my heart. What does my heart tell me about what they're saying?

The moment they begin to speak, I ask, "God, is that You?"

If He says, "Yes, that's Me," I reply, "Thank You, Lord. I'll take everything they say as though You're talking to me."

That's how you should receive prophecy. Then you'll be blessed.

Chapter 5

Divers Kinds of Tongues and Interpretation of Tongues

*T*he gift of divers kinds of tongues is a supernatural utterance in an unknown language.

Someone may argue, "I've been baptized in the Holy Spirit. I speak in tongues. So I've got one of the nine gifts." No, you don't. I said, *No, you don't!*

Divers kinds of tongues is *not* your prayer language, and your prayer language is not one of the nine gifts of the Spirit. Let me explain.

For one thing, divers tongues is not as *you* will; it's as *the Spirit* wills. That proves to me that divers kinds of tongues is not your prayer language, because you should be able to speak in tongues when you want to; but you *can't* give a message in divers kinds of tongues when you want to. It's only as the Spirit wills. Every one of the nine gifts of the Spirit is as the Spirit of God wills, not as you will.

This is an area where we're having a problem in churches today. People come to the mike and say something like, "Banana, banana, banana," and then they go sit down. They wait for the interpretation for "banana," but there's not going to be any. Do you know why? *Because it never was a "message" in the first place!* These people are simply speaking something out of their own private prayer language.

Speaking Mysteries to God

The Bible says that when you pray in an unknown tongue, you speak *mysteries* unto God (see 1 Cor. 14:2). *God doesn't want you to know what you're praying about!* It's got nothing to do with you. That's why He gives you a private prayer language: So you won't interfere with what the Spirit of God is praying through you!

If half the Christians knew what they were praying by the Spirit of God, they would quit praying. They would say, "I don't want *that*." Meanwhile, the Spirit of God is praying *the perfect will of God* for you!

To summarize, divers tongues is as *the Spirit* wills. Your prayer language is as *you* will. That's simple enough to understand.

There will also be a discernable difference in anointing between a genuine message in tongues and something spoken out of a person's prayer language.

We've got too many people getting up to give a message in tongues when it's not a message in tongues. It's not divers tongues. It's their prayer language, and they should be told it is.

When There Is No Interpretation

Every "message" in tongues doesn't need to be interpreted. Some so-called "messages" that come forth are really not messages; it's just someone worshiping God.

We must learn the things of the Spirit. We must learn how the Spirit of God flows, and whether someone is just worshiping God, or if it is a message that needs to be interpreted. Messages in divers tongues will be powerful and supernatural, and *there will always be an interpretation—always*. Unless it is given forth as a sign, the person giving the tongue should always be prepared to interpret it. Don't give a tongue if you can't give the interpretation.

That's what happens far too often. People come up to the front, give a few words in tongues, sit down, and everyone waits, looks, and wonders about the interpretation.

If it happens in my meeting, I say, "Brother, come back and give the interpretation to that."

"Oh, brother, I don't have it."

Then don't give the tongue. If you're not prepared to interpret, don't give it, because it takes the same faith to interpret that it takes to give it.

It's too easy. Anyone can come up and run off words in tongues, but giving the interpretation is another story.

Counterfeit Tongues

I've heard a lot of flakes prophesy, but I haven't heard a lot of flakes giving a divers tongue. If they do, it will only be one or two words, because the longer they give it, the more they will be exposed. *There's something about a heavenly language that you can't counterfeit.*

I was in one meeting where a woman got up, gave a message in tongues, and I ran right down the aisle, grabbed hold of her and said, "Come out, in Jesus' name!" She fell to the floor and started foaming at the mouth.

People looked at me and asked, "How did you know?"

Because the moment she gave the tongue, the Lord said, "Religious devil." The tongue wasn't from Heaven.

Did you know the devil can counterfeit tongues? Some cults believe in "tongues" and speak in "tongues."

If anyone wants to come and give a message, let him. If it's false, you'll know it a mile away, for you can't counterfeit tongues yourself. Because human beings can't counterfeit tongues, I believe it is a protection to the Church. *Tongues either come from Heaven or from hell.*

Of course, if you have been filled with the Spirit of God, you have the *Holy Spirit*, and you don't have to worry about this or be afraid of counterfeit tongues for yourself. You must be careful of strangers coming into your midst, especially in large congregations, and wanting to give a tongue or interpretation. Sometimes when you let them speak, they'll bind up the meeting and hinder the flow.

One person got up and prophesied, "I'm a God of love and a God of hate." That contradicts itself.

The Church's "Alarm System"

When a flaky person is prophesying in error, you feel sick in the pit of your stomach. You know it's not from God. It's the same when a tongue comes forth that's not of God. There's a sense of uneasiness. But when it's a heavenly language, there's a flow that brings blessing.

I believe God has set this "alarm system" of spiritual discerning in the Body of Christ. If we will learn to heed the Spirit of God, we will enter into greater things in these last days.

God wants us to get to the place where we're walking in the power of the Spirit, in the realm of the supernatural, not in a low, carnal level or realm. Church, God is calling us to move *higher* in the things of God!

A Prophecy Given by the Holy Spirit

There are higher heights and deeper depths of the Spirit of God, and many which sit on the outside and many which settle for the crumbs.

But come in and partake of the real, for there is a real. Don't be concerned about the counterfeit. Don't worry about the counterfeit, but look unto the Holy Spirit, the third Person of the Godhead, for He is the great Teacher of the Church. He will teach you all things, and He will show you all things to come.

So you will learn, you will know, you will grow up into maturity, and you will know, This is the way, walk ye in it. And you won't be confused, and you won't walk in doubt, but you will walk with the Spirit and the anointing of God. And great and mighty things will be done.

Stir yourself up. Stir yourself up in the Holy Spirit, and don't settle for the low things; but move up higher into the place that God has for you, and great shall be the blessing upon you, upon your household, and upon your congregation.

For the joy of the Lord and the glory of God shall be among you, and many shall say, "Truly, they walk in the anointing. They speak by the anointing. They talk by the anointing." And they will know it's not you. They will know it's Me, saith the Lord.

A Call to Go Higher

God is calling us higher! We must move up *higher!* We must move up into the place that God has for us. Some churches think if they have a little tongues and interpretation, God showed up. We're settling for such a *small* manifestation of the power of God!

There is a greater move of the Spirit of God available to us. There is a greater move of the Spirit of God!

Your *prayer language* is not a sign, but *divers tongues* is a sign—a sign to the unbeliever. Divers tongues is powerful when it comes forth.

Furthermore, divers tongues plus the interpretation of tongues is the equivalent of prophetic utterance.

Just before I left for the United States one time, God gave me a word of knowledge in a meeting. He said, "There's a man here with a heart problem. Tell him, 'Come here right now. God is going to heal you.' "

I gave this word, and as the man came toward me, I looked at him and said, "Sir, the Lord just spoke to me and said, 'I'll take out the stony heart and put in a heart of flesh.' God says He's going to give you a new heart." The man was deaf in both ears. He was wearing two hearing aids.

Tongues: A Sign

As I laid hands on him, the power of God came on me. I spoke several words over him, but I knew it wasn't just me praying in tongues. God touched this man; in fact, he fell out under the power of God.

I prayed for him, removed the hearing aids, and God opened both his ears! Before, he could hear just a little bit of vibration without them; after prayer, he could hear perfectly. So he fell out again! He was so drunk, he was staggering around, and they had to help him to the front seat. It turned out he was the pastor's father.

After this, a man in the congregation put his hand up.

I was a bit annoyed. After all, this wasn't a question-and-answer period. "Sir, what do you want?" I asked him.

He replied, "Brother, you spoke in an African language."

"What are you talking about?"

"When you laid hands on that man, you spoke in an African language. You spoke in Xhosa."

I might recognize one or two words of Xhosa, but I don't speak Xhosa. (My father, who was present in the service, understands Xhosa, *but he heard me speak in tongues*.)

I said, "What did I say?"

"You said, as you laid hands on him, 'God is giving you a heart as strong as a horse!' "

That hit the whole row of people who understood Xhosa! If you ask the Xhosa people what it means to have a strong heart, they will reply, "It means to have a heart like a horse." That was a sign to those people in the congregation.

A Sign to a Discouraged Missionary

Another instance of divers tongues being an actual language happened to a missionary. She had been on the mission field in India for many years, but had come home deeply discouraged. Her first Sunday back home, a woman stood up and delivered a message in tongues. The church waited for the interpretation.

The missionary was electrified by the woman's words! Finally, sobbing uncontrollably, the missionary stood and said, "There will be no interpretation to that. God was speaking to me in the dialect of the remote Indian village I've just come from. No other westerner has ever been there."

"God said to me, 'Go back. Your time is not finished. Go back in the field, and you will reap the harvest.' I'm going to obey. I'm going to go back in a few weeks, and I'm going to do what God said."

What a sign! You see, there's a realm of divers tongues that we have not walked in. We must stir ourselves up in them. We must not take prophecy, divers tongues, or interpretation lightly. If we do, it's bordering on blasphemy against the Holy Spirit!

The thing I fear more than anything else is blaspheming the Holy Spirit, or grieving the Spirit of Grace. I'd rather go on to be with Jesus right now if I knew that I would ever do that.

How to Be Used in the Utterance Gifts

If you want to be used in the utterance gifts, pray often in tongues, because Jude 20 says you build up your spirit by praying in tongues: "But ye, beloved, building up yourselves on your most holy faith, praying in the Holy Ghost." You tune your spirit into the Spirit of God by praying in the Holy Spirit.

Then, when you come into a place of meeting, or a place where God wants to use you, get ready, and you'll sense it as it starts to boil on the inside of you like a pressure cooker. The anointing will come, and you will give the tongue and move in that realm.

God wants to do many signs. In these last days, men and women of God will be speaking in English, and the Spirit of God will take their words and they will be speaking in a foreign language, and people will be touched as they listen.

Men and women of God will be in foreign countries, and through the gift of divers kinds of tongues will speak forth the word of God. They will be speaking English, but their listeners will hear them speak perfect Russian, perfect Italian, perfect Chinese, and so forth. (See Acts 2:4-11.)

They will think, *Oh, I spoke a lovely message in English*, but the people will hear them in their own language, just like the Day of Pentecost: "And they...began to speak with other tongues.... Every man heard them speak in his own language" (Acts 2:4,6). The Holy Spirit changed the words in midair, so to speak! It was a sign to touch people.

Interpretation of Tongues

Now let's look at the supernatural gift of interpretation of tongues. *It is a showing forth by the Holy Spirit the meaning of the utterance in other tongues.* It is an *interpretation* of what was said, not a *translation*. You're not translating what was said in tongues word for word.

This explains why someone can give a *message in tongues* that lasts for two minutes, yet *the interpretation* lasts for thirty seconds. It's because they are interpreting what was said by the Spirit of God; they are not translating it.

If you spoke a sentence in Italian, and I translated it into English, it would probably take the same amount of time. However, if I simply shared the general meaning of what you said, it might be shorter.

The Bible says in First Corinthians 14:13, "Wherefore let him that speaketh in an unknown tongue pray that he may interpret." If no one is present who can interpret, pray that you yourself can interpret. Say, "God, give me the interpretation to that."

Every time I hear a tongue, I pray to give the interpretation; I don't care who gave the tongue. I pray, "God, give *me* the interpretation!" Sometimes I'll get it and someone else will give it, and it will be exactly what I got. Then I say, "Hallelujah! Thank You, Jesus!" That's how you can train yourself. Just remember, divers tongues and the interpretation of tongues is equivalent to prophecy. In other words divers kinds of tongues needs interpretation of tongues, unless it is a sign, as mentioned previously.

Desire the Gifts

Desire, desire, desire the gifts! *Desire* to prophesy. *Desire* to operate in the gifts—not for your glory; for God's glory. Wait on the Holy Spirit for the gifts to operate in your life.

It's especially wonderful when you see a couple operating in divers tongues and interpretation. The wife will give the tongue and the husband the interpretation, or the husband will give the tongue and the wife the interpretation. Sometimes God will use my wife and me that way. God will give her the tongue and give me the interpretation, and we'll flow together.

> Desire, desire, desire the gifts!...Desire to prophesy. Desire to operate in the gifts—not for your glory; for God's glory.

You can begin to believe God for that manifestation in your own life. Begin to pray, "God, use us in that area. We desire to be used in the gifts—not to lift us up, but to touch people." *Covet earnestly the best gifts.*

Don't Quench the Spirit

But remember: "The spirits of the prophets are subject to the prophets" (1 Cor. 14:32). In other words, the anointing can come on you, and you *can* quench it. You can always quench the anointing.

How many times have you been in a service and the power of God has come on you and you felt it, but you pushed it away? Where are those tongues and interpretations? Where are those prophecies that should have come forth from you?

Your excuse may have been, "I was worried. What if the congregation wouldn't receive it?"

If it's God, they *have* to receive it! Why? *Because the anointing will be there!* You need to exercise the gifts of the Spirit when that anointing falls on you.

Let me explain to you what really happens when the anointing comes on you and you don't flow with it. Let's say the anointing falls on Brother Jones. God is stirring him up to begin to move in the gifts of the Spirit. But Brother Jones says, "No, God. I don't want to be used in the gifts of the Spirit."

So the Spirit of God keeps looking and searching for people who will yield to Him. He comes over to Sister Smith, but she says, "No, God, not today. I did that last week. What will they think of me?"

So the Spirit of God goes to Sister Brown, and she says, "Yes, Lord," and she gets up and gives the word of the Lord.

Next Sunday, the anointing of the Spirit comes back to Brother Jones, and again he says, "No, God. I don't want to be used in the gifts." It jumps back to Sister Smith and again she says, "No, God, not today." It goes back to Sister Brown, and she gives the message.

People will ask, "Why is *she* giving a message again this week?" Because she yielded again. Because God spoke to five other people, and they all refused!

Three or four weeks later, the Spirit of God doesn't come to Brother Jones or Sister Smith anymore. They wonder, "Why doesn't God use me anymore? I don't feel that anointing anymore. I don't feel the presence of God anymore. My heart doesn't pound like I know I've got to speak."

It's because God knows you won't give the message, but He knows Sister Brown *will*, so He keeps going to her. And everyone criticizes Sister Brown. "She's *always* giving messages and prophesying!"

It's not because she's "always"; it's because she's *yielded*!

The Reason Believers Don't Obey

Many of you have felt the anointing of God. You've suddenly felt like someone poured a hot shower on you.

Your whole body has been burning like fire. Your heart has been pounding, and you've had the word of the Lord burning in your belly. Yet you've stayed put.

You need to be rebuked because you're afraid! The reason you don't want to yield to the gifts is because you're scared of getting in the flesh—because you *are* in the flesh. When you are in the Spirit, fear goes—boldness comes. You don't even think of sinking. You end up walking on the water.

I'd rather have ten people get up, prophesy, and make a mistake, but keep trying, wanting to excel in the things of God, than have hundreds of people sit there and criticize—when all of them can be used of God.

Stir yourselves up! When that anointing comes, wait for the right time to deliver the word of the Lord. Sometimes I've held a prophecy for two weeks!

I'd been in a service with thousands of people, and I knew the preacher, so I said, "God, he has the Spirit of God, so if what I've got to say is so important, You get him to call me out."

And that preacher looked up at me and said, "Brother Rodney, come up here. You have the word of the Lord." And I went up there on the platform and delivered the word of the Lord.

"Give It to Me Again"

In situations like that, when I have to hold a prophecy, I always let the Lord give it to me about three times; not that I am resisting. I say, "God, if that's You, give it to me again." I put it aside and it will come again. I put it aside once more, and it will come again. Then I know it's God, because I wasn't thinking about it.

That's how I know about the word of knowledge and the word of wisdom, too. The word of the Lord will come to me, and God will say this, that, and the other. And I'll say, "God, if that's You, give it to me again." And He'll give it to me again. I'll push it aside, all the time keeping my spiritual ear tuned to His voice, and He'll give it to me again. Then I'll know it's God, and I'll flow with it.

So we must stir ourselves up in the gifts. And the way to do that for the utterance gifts is to pray in other tongues. However, we must understand this: Every time you pray in tongues, you are not interceding. You are praying in tongues. You make the decision to pray in tongues. There is a big difference between the spirit of intercession and just praying in the Spirit. Praying in the Spirit comes as an act of your will. The spirit of intercession comes by the Holy Spirit as He wills.

When many people pray in the Spirit, they aren't concentrating on building themselves up; they're wondering who they're praying for. Maybe I'm praying for someone in China, they think. No, you're just building yourself up!

You're tuning your spirit into the wavelength of the Holy Spirit. You're quieting down all the other voices, and you're tuning your spirit into the wavelength of the Spirit of God so you can hear His voice.

Part Three

The Gifts of Power

Chapter 6

The Gift of Faith

In this section, we will look closely at the supernatural gifts of power. These are the three gifts that do something:

1. The gift of faith
2. The working of miracles
3. The gift of healing(s)

Our text from First Corinthians 12 tells us there are diversities of gifts, differences of administrations, and diversities of operations, "...but it is the same God which worketh all in all" (verse 6).

After naming all nine gifts of the Spirit, Paul pointed out in verse 11, "But all these worketh that one and the selfsame Spirit, dividing to every man severally as He will."

We will begin by examining the gift of faith. I believe there are many misconceptions about this gift. People need to have a revelation concerning the gift of faith.

Faith Defined

First, let's begin by defining the gift of faith. *The gift of faith is a divine supernatural manifestation of God's* *faith imparted to you at a specific time, at a specific place, for a specific purpose. It is the supernatural gift from God to receive a miracle.*

The supernatural gift of faith, however, has nothing to do with the type of simple faith that comes "...by hearing, and hearing by the word of God" (Rom. 10:17).

The best way I can describe it is to liken your whole being to a pop bottle. When you unscrew the cap and pour the contents out, that's what God does when He comes to you. It's almost like He unscrews your head—I wish He'd leave some people's heads off permanently—and He pours all of *you* out.

He empties all the doubt, unbelief, and everything else that hinders faith, and He reaches up on the shelf and grabs the jug marked "God's Faith." He pours His faith into you right to the brim, puts your head back on, and you are now full of super-duper, high-octane, unleaded God's faith!

> He empties all the doubt, unbelief, and everything else that hinders faith, and He... pours His faith into you....

You can run around on His faith for however long that gift is on you. Supernatural things will begin to happen, because God imparted faith to you. When you speak something, it comes to pass.

Supernatural Faith

But when the gift lifts, you say, "What happened? That wasn't me!" No, it wasn't you; it was God. God's faith can come on you at any time of the day or night—at two o'clock in the morning or whenever. Yes, I believe you must build your faith in the Word of God, but there *is* such a thing as the supernatural gift of faith.

When the supernatural gift of faith comes on you, and you begin to move in that area, you will begin to scare everyone! Why? Because you're not operating in the natural realm anymore. You're operating with God's faith.

If you want to walk with Jesus, go read Matthew, Mark, Luke, and John. Walk with Jesus through the pages of the Gospels and see what happened when He said to the people, "Roll away the stone." I tell you, Peter was already trying to find another job. Thomas was saying, "I don't believe this." And Judas was probably picking the pockets of the people in the crowd!

When you are clothed or anointed with supernatural faith, such Holy Spirit-inspired boldness comes on you that the devils of hell begin to tremble! People know that when you speak the Word of God, it will come to pass—not because you said it, but because God's faith is involved in it.

Some people think that this supernatural gift of faith is something you can work toward. No, you can't. You've either got it, or you haven't.

The gift of faith is not some little weak thing; it's a power gift. It's a miraculous gift from God. It's God's ability—*God's power to receive miracles!*

Now Peter and John went up together into the temple at the hour of prayer, being the ninth hour. And a certain man lame from his mother's womb was carried, whom they laid daily at the gate of the temple...to ask alms of them that entered into the temple; who seeing Peter and John about to go into the temple asked an alms. And Peter, fastening his eyes upon him with John, said, Look on us. And he gave heed unto them, expecting to receive something of them. Then Peter said, Silver and gold have I none; but such as I have give I thee: In the name of Jesus Christ of Nazareth rise up and walk (Acts 3:1-6).

Such as I Have: God's Faith

What was it: natural faith, or God's faith? It was God's faith. Peter walked up to the lame man, and the power of God fell on him—the supernatural gift of faith fell on him—he spoke the word of God, and it came to pass.

When the gift of faith comes on you, whatever it is you're praying for will come to pass! It's almost impossible for the gift of faith to come on you and *not* have something happen, because you are operating in God's faith, and you can do anything in God's faith! Do you realize that? It's wonderful. It's beautiful. And you get to sit back and watch it happen.

Daniel received a miracle by the gift of faith. When he was thrown into that lions' den, he didn't have time to get his confession pact out. His faith either worked, or it didn't!

There are times when you don't have faith for something yourself, and there are times when God's faith will come on you. Some of you have been operating in the gift of faith, but you haven't realized it. You're going to understand this for the first time now.

Carried on God's Faith

Have you ever been through a two-week period when everything you said suddenly happened, and everything you did worked? Then, two weeks later, your seeming success was gone, and you wondered if you were still saved. You thought, *Maybe I should read my Bible more. Maybe I should pray more.*

What really happened to you? You didn't realize that God was carrying you on *His* faith for a while. I know the feeling.

God sometimes drops the supernatural gift of faith on certain people to believe Him supernaturally for finances.

How many of you know the story of George Mueller? He had a number of orphanages in England many years ago, and he believed God for food and money to take care of hundreds of children. He wouldn't tell anyone his needs; he'd just pray, and people would bring or send food and money.

Today people think faith without *hints* is dead. Today people think if you have a need, let your request be made known unto men—but the Bible says let your request be made known unto God. We've got a lot of "faith hinters" around.

They'll come and stand in the foyer, praying, "O God, Thou knowest I need new shoes, size 9½, God." When it comes to pass, they declare, "Oh, my faith brought it in!" No, your big mouth brought it in because someone felt sorry for you.

Faith for Daily Food

Elijah, in First Kings 17, received a miracle by the gift of faith when the ravens brought him a hamburger every day. Well, the Bible actually says the ravens brought him bread and flesh in the morning and again at night. Isn't bread and flesh a kind of hamburger? Maybe it was a double cheeseburger, and the raven got the cheese.

Regardless, it took supernatural faith. If you don't believe that, go down to the nearest river and wait there all day and see if a raven brings *you* bread and meat. Some people would be fortunate if God brought them anything. Elijah was operating in God's faith.

Wigglesworth: Bold Apostle of Faith

Smith Wigglesworth was what you might call "an apostle of faith." He was a bold man. Those who knew him say he never read anything but the Bible.

He had been an illiterate plumber who got so busy preaching, he couldn't plumb anymore. His wife, who was in the ministry before he was, taught him to read. His ministry began when he was 56 years old, and it lasted until he was nearly 88—more than 30 years. During that time, about 20 people were raised from the dead under his ministry. Although Wigglesworth was bold and tenacious, it wasn't natural faith he was operating in; it was God's faith.

He was a wild man! He scared the devil and hell out of all the religious people of his day. For example, if a person came twice in his healing line, he'd kick him off the platform. He'd literally turn the man around, kick him in the seat of the pants, and the guy would go flying off the platform—crutches and all—and get up healed.

One night they brought a man who was dying of cancer to Wigglesworth's healing line. They said, "Brother Wigglesworth, this man is dying of cancer."

Dying to Be Healed

Wigglesworth punched him in the stomach so hard he flew through the air and hit the floor, dead! He killed him! So they came running to Wigglesworth and said, "He's *dead*, Brother Wigglesworth!"

He looked at them and said in his clipped English accent, "He's healed."

Ten minutes later, the man was up and running around the church. Wigglesworth could do that, but you can't go around hitting people when you pray for them. God has to tell you when to do it!

Sometimes when a deaf person has stood in front of me, before I knew it, my right hand has come up and slapped them. They fell flat on the floor, and they got up totally healed by the power of God.

Sometimes before a person could even close his or her eyes, I've slapped them flat on the head, fast as a six-gun draw! And they got up healed by the power of God. Afterwards, when I've asked them, "Did you feel me hit you?" they've insisted, "You didn't hit me." Before my hand touched them, the power of God hit them and did that miracle.

Chapter 7

The Power Gift Twins

You will find that the gift of faith and the working of miracles work together, because when the gift of faith comes along, the working of miracles comes with it. They're like twins—they flow together. They are the twins of the power gifts.

The gift of working miracles is a supernatural gift from God. It is an impartation of God's faith to work and perform miracles instantaneously. It is a divine manifestation of God's power imparted to you at a specific time, at a specific place, for a specific purpose.

Once, it is said, Smith Wigglesworth stayed with a preacher who had no feet, just stumps. Wigglesworth instructed the man, "Tomorrow morning at eight o'clock, go down to the shoe shop and buy yourself a brand-new pair of shoes."

The man recognized the power of God operating through Wigglesworth's life, so he didn't argue. When you get around anointed people and they tell you to do something, you'd better do it; especially if they add a "Thus saith the Lord."

So the next morning at eight o'clock, the minister made his way down to the shoe store on his crutches and told the clerk, "I need a pair of shoes," and he told him the size and color he wanted.

The clerk looked at the man's stumps and started to say, "But, sir...." The minister said, "Don't but...give me the shoes." The clerk returned with the shoes. The minister took the first shoe, and as he put it over his wooden stump, flesh formed. The remainder of his leg formed, and a foot was created! Then he took the other shoe, and his other leg was lengthened and a foot was added. He went to get new shoes, and he got new feet! Wigglesworth spoke that by the gift of faith.

How to Raise the Dead

Many want to know how to raise the dead. One man joked, "I can't get my wife out of bed in the morning, let alone raise the dead."

You're going to need three gifts working together to raise the dead. That's why we don't see many people raised from the dead in this day and age.

I'm serious about this: Some people are better left dead. If you think I'm being too hard, notice that Jesus didn't raise every dead person He encountered as He walked the dusty roads of the Holy Land. Sometimes people are better off going home to be with the Lord.

First, you're going to need the gift of faith to raise the dead, because it's beyond natural faith. If you don't believe it, go to the mortuary, find a corpse, and see how you do.

Second, you're going to need the gift of working of miracles, because raising the dead is a working of miracles.

Third, you're going to need the gifts of healings to get the person healed from the thing he died from. Otherwise, when you'd raise him from the dead, he'd just drop dead again from the same disease, illness, or injury that killed him the first time.

You need these three gifts in operation to raise the dead. And it's *as the Spirit wills.*

When I hear that someone is dying, and I know I can go pray for this person, I first ask, "God, what do You want me to do?" If the Lord says, "Nothing," I don't worry about it.

Waiting for Miracles

But I'm waiting for the day to come when the anointing will come back to the Church—when men and women of God will once again walk in the power of God, and the miracles that were seen after the Day of Pentecost will be seen once more.

The days of miracles are not over! The day will come in this last-day outpouring of the Spirit of God when we'll see even *greater* miracles than those stumps that were transformed by the power of God.

The day will come when the dead will be raised, and signs and wonders will be seen in whole communities. The blind, the maimed, the brain-damaged, and other afflicted people who are well known in their communities will be raised off their beds by the power of God, and they will touch whole nations.

We're entering into that time when supernatural signs and wonders will be done by the power of God. However, such a time is not for the fearful. If you're afraid of some of the things that are happening now and will continue to happen in meetings, it's not for you. You need to get into the "meat," the strong things of God.

Receive the Fresh Anointing

There is a deeper realm of the Spirit of God. The days of playing church are over. We've got to press on into the deeper things and receive the fresh anointing that God would pour out in the new century.

It's going to be different, it's going to astound and stagger religious people, and it's going to make the devil mad. But we're going to see a great manifestation of the glory of God and the gift of faith—and ordinary lay people will be used supernaturally in the gift of faith.

The gift of faith will be used in the area of protection. For example, suppose you're driving down the highway when a car suddenly appears out of nowhere, heading straight for you! You say, "In the name of Jesus!" and not a hair of your head is touched. God will protect you.

That's how the gift of faith works. Suddenly you need it, and it's there. Isn't that exciting? We're going to see the gift of faith come into operation more and more.

We don't have to fear in these days when terror and evil are going on all around us. Nothing shall come nigh us, for we are covered by the blood of Jesus.

If you're walking as a carnal Christian and these gifts aren't available to you, you'd better get worried enough to ask an anointed person to help you.

Another way the gift of faith is used is in casting out devils. You can look directly at the demon-possessed person and say, "Come out, in Jesus' name!" and he won't sit there screaming for three more hours; he'll be delivered! You'll just speak it by the Spirit of God.

When Jesus spoke to the man who was bound with chains in the graveyard, the demons in him said, "[We are] Legion: for we are many" (Mk. 5:9b). Then they asked permission to go into the swine, and Jesus said, "Go." How did Jesus do that? By the gift of faith.

The gift of faith also comes into operation through laying hands on people. This is an area we take too lightly. The laying on of hands is for impartation. You can receive things by the laying on of hands; anointings can be imparted to you by the gift of faith.

Expect the Supernatural

When you get stirred up in the area of the gifts, you'll be driving down the highway, suddenly the word of the Lord will come to you, and you'll just *know* something, and things will begin to happen in your life—supernatural things. If you're not expecting the supernatural to happen, it won't. But if you're expecting it, it will. Why? Because God wants to use every one of us in this end-time revival.

> If you're not expecting the supernatural to happen, it won't. But if you're expecting it, it will.

The gift of faith can be used in subduing storms. Jesus stood up in that boat on the Sea of Galilee and rebuked the wind and the waves. He said, "Peace, be still!" As we saw, the gift of faith and the working of miracles often overlap; they're linked together.

There's a time when you can lay hands on people by natural faith, but sometimes the gift of faith comes into operation as the word of the Lord comes. For example, you're looking over the congregation, and God says, "That person—come here right now."

God tells you all about the person, you give him a word, and the gift of faith comes into operation. You speak the word, and it happens in the time that God appointed. The gift of faith is not something you dreamed up; it's there.

You ask, "How will I know that I have the gift of faith?"

You'll know it and everyone around you will know it, because everyone with doubt and unbelief will leave. And, when the gift of faith lifts, you'll be astounded. You'll say, "My, my, that wasn't me, was it?" And everyone will agree, "No, it wasn't you."

Chapter 8

The Working of Miracles

The working of miracles is a supernatural gift from God to work a miracle. It is an intervention of God in the course of nature.

In other words, the working of a miracle is the sun and moon standing still. It is dividing the Red Sea, turning water into wine, or feeding five thousand people with five loaves and two fishes. It is walking on water.

If you don't believe that walking on water is a miracle, fill up your bathtub or swimming pool, and let's see how you do walking on water.

Unfortunately, we're living in a day and an age when people no longer believe in miracles. I heard one preacher say that a satellite was a miracle.

No, the satellite wasn't a miracle. It was one of man's technological advances. Man put it there; God never put it there. Of course, if a man stood and said, "Satellite—be!" and suddenly there was a satellite, it would be a miracle, wouldn't it?

People look at a sunset and say, "Oh, what a wonderful miracle!" No, the sunset is not a miracle. The sun rises in the east and sets in the west every day. There's nothing miraculous about it. It's normal. If sunsets were miracles, everyone in Hawaii would get saved!

There are always people trying to explain away miracles. If five deaf people out of ten walked away from a healing line totally healed, the critics wouldn't look at them; they'd focus on the five who *weren't* healed. Critics, I'm convinced, are direct descendants of Thomas the Doubter, the unbelieving one.

One theologian was trying to explain away the parting of the Red Sea. He said, "That wasn't such a great miracle. Scientists have found that a certain part of this sea was only five inches deep."

One of his students put up his hand and said, "Why, Mr. Theologian, that makes it an even *greater* miracle, because it means God drowned the whole Egyptian army in five inches of water!"

Another bright fellow tried to explain away the miracle of the loaves and fishes. He said, "The miracle of the five loaves and two fishes wasn't such a great miracle, for as we study in history, we find that they had very big loaves of bread in those days."

Lunch: One Whale

He forgot it was lunch for one little boy! Can't you just hear the lad's mother: "Where are you going, Johnny?"

"I'm going to lunch."

So she packs him five huge loaves. And a whale.

God made the Word of God so simple, *you need an idiot to help you misunderstand it.*

What is the purpose of a miracle? To display God's power and magnificence. It means "the working of impelling, staggering wonders or astonishments."

Acts 5:12 reports, "And by the hands of the apostles were many signs and wonders wrought..."

> God made the Word of God so simple, you need an idiot to help you misunderstand it.

On one occasion during my first year of full-time ministry, I had been preaching for about ten minutes in a Methodist church when the Lord said to me, "There's a man here and his one leg is shorter than the other." So I stopped preaching and said, "God just spoke to me and said there's a man here whose one leg is shorter than the other. Would you please come up here?"

When the man stepped out into the aisle in plain view, I nearly fainted! His one leg was a whole three and a half inches shorter than the other.

I thought to myself, *O my God, I've blown it! I'm in big trouble now! I'm finished. My ministry is over. It hasn't even begun, but now it's over. These people are going to stone me, or take me out in the desert and leave me to shrivel up in the sun. I'm going to come back looking like a California raisin or something!*

When I looked at this man's leg in the natural, I didn't want to pray for him. I wanted someone else to pray for him. Or I wanted to make some excuse. I wanted to tell him something spiritual, like, "Go thy way and speak the Word for ten weeks."

But as he came and stood in front of me, something suddenly fell on me. It was like someone dropped a coat on me. I turned to the congregation and said, "If you want to see a miracle, get up here"—but my mind was saying, "What are you talking about!"

"Shut up!" I told my mind, and I asked the man to be seated on a chair. The heel on his built-up shoe was three and a half inches high. And you can't fake that.

I sat down facing him, and the gift of faith and the working of miracles fell on me. All I said was, "In the name of Je..." I was about to say "Jesus," but I only got as far as the first syllable when the power of God hit this Methodist fellow in the top of his head and went right down into his feet.

His short leg shot out to match the normal-sized leg, and the man burst out in other tongues as he was baptized in the Holy Spirit. He had to remove his shoes and walk home barefooted because his special pair of shoes was no longer of use to him.

You can't *make* that kind of thing happen. You can believe God for it, but you can't make it happen. If we could, we'd break the "switch" for this gift and keep it on all night!

The Peril of Power

Let's suppose the gift of working of miracles and the gift of faith came into a service and remained for several hours. People would be rushing to the hospitals and bringing people to the church.

If a preacher had the gift of faith working in an unlimited degree in his life along with the working of miracles, people would break down the door of his house to get in.

People with AIDS would come, people in wheelchairs would come, people who are blind would come, and people would fly in from other countries. That's why we don't see the power gifts in manifestation: God couldn't entrust that type of power to man, because man would foul it up and merchandise the anointing, using it to make money. And God is not going to share His glory with anyone.

The same year I prayed for the Methodist man, I was in the Transkei, Southern Africa, preaching in a hut with a cow dung floor. About two hundred people were packed into that hut, and I preached on miracles.

The first person to come up in the healing line was a mother holding a little child whose club feet were locked in calipers. I thought, *O God, not her first, please! Let me pray for headaches first.* But I said, "Take those calipers off." I held the baby's feet in my hands, and as I said, "Father, in the name of Jesus...," the legs swung around right in my hands.

My interpreter, an African man, said, "I've never seen anything like this before!" and he dropped flat on his face, weeping. God gave that child an instant miracle. Let me tell you, we had a revival!

Someone said, "I've never seen a deaf ear opened."

How many deaf ears have you prayed for?

"None."

That figures.

"I've never seen a dead person raised, Brother Rodney."

How many dead have you prayed for?

"None."

That makes sense, doesn't it?

You say, "I've never seen any blind eyes opened."

How many blind eyes have you prayed for?

A Shaky Beginning

I think for the first two years of my ministry, most of the people I prayed for that had terminal diseases died. Don't blame *me*! They were about to die anyway; they just happened to stop by me as a last resort. And I was only learning how to pray for the sick, you know.

But as I continued to be faithful and obey God, following the anointing, God began to move in an even greater way in my life.

God wants to see if you'll be faithful to continue to pray for people, regardless, or if your faith in God's ability will waver, and you will end up compromising what you *really* believe in order to become acceptable to those around you.

When I made the decision, "I'll not compromise even if it means never being invited to speak at some churches or meetings," that's when the blessing of God began to flow in my ministry in a way I never dreamed it could. And all glory goes unto His majestic name.

If you want the miraculous, you have to make a decision not to compromise, and to contend for the supernatural. Be bold!

Chapter 9

Gift of Healing(s)

The gift of healing(s) is a supernatural intervention of God's healing power over sickness and diseases without natural means.

Sometimes God uses certain people in the healing of certain sicknesses and diseases. I don't know why. If one person had it all, we could just go to him. But since one person doesn't have it all, that's why we need all the members of the Body of Christ moving together in the supernatural things of God.

God often uses me in the area of deaf ears and cancer cases. I don't know why. Many cancer cases are healed through my ministry, and sometimes arthritis. I'd rather pray for a deaf ear any day before I'd pray for a blind eye, yet I've had blind eyes opened in my meetings, too.

I was holding a meeting once in Louisville, Kentucky, and a totally blind girl was led in. She was carrying a white cane. The power of God came into that place and blew a whole row of people out on the floor. They were down there laughing in the Spirit.

After 45 minutes, the blind girl began to shout and scream, "I can see! I can see!" She got up and ran around the room. She could describe how many fingers I was holding up in front of her, what I was wearing, and so forth.

One night in New York City, right in the Bronx, 18 deaf ears opened instantly—18 in a row. I know it had absolutely nothing to do with me!

Whenever God uses you, you must realize it's God; it's not you. All you've got to do is make yourself available for Him to flow through you. If we could make it happen—if we could turn the switch on to make it happen—we'd keep it on all the time.

Healings vs. Miracles

There is a difference between healings and miracles. A healing is the removal of sicknesses or diseases in parts of the body, whereas a miracle is creative.

In other words, a miracle is when an eyeball is formed in an empty eye socket, an arm grows back, or organs are replaced. That's miraculous. And miracles are instant.

> A healing is the removal of sicknesses or diseases in parts of the body, whereas a miracle is creative.

A healing can also be instant, or it can manifest gradually. When you get prayed for in a healing line and you don't see an immediate change, don't go away thinking you didn't get your healing.

Some people don't need healing; they need a miracle. If half of a man's stomach is eaten away with cancer, he doesn't need a healing; he's not sick. Half his stomach is gone. He needs a miracle! If he had a miracle, he wouldn't have a problem.

Creative Miracles

It's the same with people who are brain damaged. They don't need a healing, for they aren't sick. They need a miracle— a creative miracle.

One man came to my service in a wheelchair, because a big tree had fallen on him and broken his back. The man was totally well, but everyone thought he was sick. I said to the people, "This brother is not sick. There's nothing wrong with him. He just needs a miracle to join those severed nerves back together."

Sometimes a healing anointing comes into services. At other times the power of God to work miracles comes.

Do you want to be used by God in the area of healings and miracles? You're not going to see healings and miracles if you don't step out on the water and start praying for people. Lay your hands on people's heads.

"What do I do then?"

Say, "In the name of Jesus!"

Find a head, lay hands on it, and say, "In the name of Jesus!" It's not difficult, but most Christians don't want to do it because they're worried about their reputation.

"What if I pray for them and they're not healed?" they fret.

What if you pray for them and they *are* healed?

A great American evangelist was asked, "What would you do if you were in the healing line and someone dropped dead right there?"

He replied, "I'd say, 'Next, please.'"

The Coming Restoration

The power gifts are going to be restored to the Church. A restoration of the working of miracles, the gift of healing(s), and the gift of faith is coming as we've never seen them before.

Even in the realm of the gift of faith, when this gift works with the working of miracles, people can have a miracle of healing as they sit in the service without any minister laying hands on them.

People riding on buses to Kathryn Kuhlman's meetings would get healed before they got to the services. Miracles would take place! People would throw away their crutches before the services even started. An old drunk walking by the auditorium could be healed by just getting in the breeze of the front doors.

It is said that people staying on nearby floors in the same hotel as Miss Kuhlman were healed and miracles happened during the night, so great was the miracle power of God.

This sounds like the days of the apostles, when people were healed when the apostles' shadows passed over them. Those days, I tell you by the Spirit of God, will come back to the Church!

The Condition of the Church

The Church is so sick and so weak, if the apostle Paul were to visit some congregations, he'd say, "You call *that* a church?"

The Church is in a pitiful shape compared with what the Book of Acts tells us we can do and be. What some people call "church" is an excuse.

It's like the story of the young man who was standing outside the door of a church, weeping. He had long hair. Jesus walked up to him and said, "Son, what's wrong?"

He said, "Jesus, I can't get in this church. They won't let me in because of my long hair."

Jesus said, "Son, I wouldn't worry about it. I've been trying to get in this church myself for the last 15 years."

Everything is very polished in some churches. They get up and sing three hymns and three hers; take up the offering; the preacher preaches from *Encyclopedia Britannica* and the *Reader's Digest*; and they pronounce the last rites... I mean, the benediction; and everyone goes home.

No one got saved, no one got healed, no one got delivered, no one got set free. If the power of God was there, you would need a magnifying glass or a microscope to find it. The only life in the whole building was the ivy growing on the walls outside.

Getting Back to the Power

We must get back to the power! You ask, "How do I do that?"

By getting hungry for God, by promising, "God, I'll change," and by throwing your religious doubts away. Instead, flow with the Holy Spirit, believe God, and see what He will do.

The definition of the supernatural gift of healing(s) is: a supernatural intervention of God's healing power over sickness and disease without natural means. In other words, no medicine and doctors.

There are remote places on earth where there are no doctors. If you get bitten by a poisonous snake, you've go no time to get a serum. You'd better believe God for your healing; otherwise, you're going home to Heaven in four minutes!

I'm not against doctors and medicine. Thank God for doctors, and thank God for medicine. If it weren't for doctors and medicine, most Christians would be dead.

Don't Get Sick in America

Just don't get sick in America. You need medical insurance. The doctors and the hospitals are taking people to the cleaners. If you get sick and spend at least two weeks in a hospital, you're looking at a minimum of $25,000. And if you have no medical insurance, you're finished!

I've never seen as many sick people as there are in the United States! If you call a healing line, 70 or 80 percent of the church will come. I've never seen anything like it!

Some cities have a high incidence of cancer because of such environmental problems as crop spraying, acid rain, and nuclear contamination. And there are other problems at work in society.

One night in the Bronx I prayed for seven people who had AIDS. You have to have the power of God to meet these situations. The Church needs to rise up with a solution.

I don't know what it's going to be like in the future concerning medical care in the United States, but right now it's going in the direction of either believe God for your healing or die!

In these last days, if we don't believe in the power of God and in signs, wonders, and miracles, we're finished. I'm not trying to be hard; I'm just saying if your faith is in going to a doctor, fine. If you've got the faith to believe in the medicine, fine. God bless you.

Jesus: The Alternative

I'm just pointing out to you that there is an alternative: The same Jesus who walked the shores of Galilee two thousand years ago is right here in the new century to do a work in your life and to change you.

He's the same Jesus who opened the eyes of the blind, the same Jesus who raised Lazarus from the dead, the same

Jesus who walked on the water, the same Jesus who fed the five thousand.

People don't want to believe! "I don't have to believe God. I've got a doctor."

They'll do whatever their doctor says: A red pill in the morning and a blue pill at night.

"Why do you take the pills?"

"The doctor said to take them."

"What does the Bible say?"

"I know what the Bible says, but the doctor said...and he knows more than the Bible."

People want to be sick. "I've worked hard for my nervous breakdown," they say. "I've earned it. I've waited for it all my life. I'm going to enjoy it, and no one's going to stop me!"

If all you talk is sickness, disease, poverty, depression, lack, and failure, that's all you're going to have in your life. And that's all some of you talk about. Start talking Jesus!

Doing the Works of Jesus

What is the purpose of the gift of healing(s)? To deliver the sick and to destroy the works of the devil. Those are the things Jesus did while He was on earth, according to Acts 10:38: "How God anointed Jesus of Nazareth with the Holy Ghost and with power: who went about doing good, and healing all that were oppressed of the devil; for God was with Him."

We saw that there are divers operations and manifestations of the gift of healing(s), for God uses different people in different areas of healing. Some have more success with cancers and tumors, some with ear problems, and others with arthritis.

To see these gifts in operation, you must come to services with a sense of expectancy. Don't sit there like a bump on a log! Do you realize you can get healed right in your seat?

Someone said, "Brother Rodney, I can't come to the healing service tonight. I'm *sick*."

What Do You Expect?

Why do you think we're having the healing service? You can get healed. You will get what you expect. Unfortunately, some people come expecting nothing.

One reason we don't see the power gifts is because we don't expect to see them. Another reason is because there are ministers who have so comprised their life and ministry, they no longer have the power of God. These things need to be said.

But the day is coming when we are going to see incurable diseases being healed, right in front of our eyes. We must contend for these things. We must go after these things. We can't be timid about them; we must be bold!

Another reason why we don't see miracles, signs, and wonders today is because many Christians are in so much doubt and unbelief. They come to a service and say, "Well, let's see what the preacher can do today."

People don't expect to see the power of God. But in these last days, we *are* going to see it!

Part Four

The Gifts of Revelation

Chapter 10

The Revelation Gifts

In this section, we are going to look at the revelation gifts. These are the gifts set in the Church by the Lord Jesus Christ to reveal things. When they begin to operate, you will *know* things.

The three revelation gifts are:

1. The word of knowledge
2. The word of wisdom
3. Discerning of spirits

Many people assume that these revelation gifts are some kind of an "inkling" or "hunch" you have, and that's how you know things.

No, when the revelation gifts flow, *knowledge* flows. And it's not natural knowledge; it's *supernatural* knowledge.

Someone asks, "How will I know when I get a word of knowledge?"

You'll know. That's what *a word of knowledge* is: *knowing.*

"How will I know when I get a word of wisdom?"

You'll know, because *a word of wisdom* is *revelation.* It comes by revelation. It comes by the Holy Spirit.

You see, the Spirit of the Living God is omniscient. The Holy Spirit knows *everything.* What happens is this: *He gives you a small portion of His knowledge through the revelation gifts.*

God Shares His Knowledge With Man

These facts in the mind of God are imparted into the hearts and minds of men pertaining to people, places, events, and things that are taking place now, things that have happened in the past, or things that will take place in the future.

When the revelation gifts are in manifestation, the Holy Spirit allows you to *see and know things in the realm of the spirit.* In other words, you can look right at someone and know spiritual and natural things about him without even talking to him. You just know it. It pops up on the inside of your belly like a pop-up toaster. You look at someone: pop, and you know!

> When the revelation gifts are in manifestation, the Holy Spirit allows you to... look right at someone and know spiritual and natural things about him without even talking to him.

Recently as I was ministering, I kept looking at the pastor. Pop—the Scripture came to me about making his tongue as "the pen of a ready writer" (Ps. 45:1b). I couldn't get away from it. It just kept on coming, and I knew I had to give it. That's how God will tell you things pertaining to people's lives.

God is talking to us many times, but we push the Spirit of God aside. We must be sensitive to the moving of the Spirit. We must begin to listen to His voice, so we'll know when He speaks to us.

Have things ever happened in your life, and you knew they were going to happen, but you did nothing about it? God was telling you before it happened, because God wants you to know what's going to happen.

No Surprises in God

Nothing should take a child of God unawares—nothing. We're not walking according to natural knowledge; we're walking according to the realm of the supernatural. *We have God's knowledge available to us!*

Nothing need take us unawares. When something happens, we should say, "Well, I knew it was going to happen. God told me it was going to happen." When you know what's coming down the pipeline, it's fun, because then you're ready for it.

Christians who will not walk by the supernatural gifts of the Spirit are not going to know what's going to hit them in the last days.

But those who will hook up to the Spirit of God—those who will be sensitive to His voice—those who will have the revelation gifts of the Spirit in manifestation—will be warned beforehand by God of things that are going to happen, not just in the church setting, but in their *everyday* life: their home, their marriage, their finances, their workplace. And when you're ministering to people, you'll know things about them, and you'll be able to help them.

The bottom line is: *All the gifts are to help people.* God didn't put the gifts in the Church to harm people. God put the gifts there to help people.

Whenever you start talking about the revelation gifts, people start getting afraid. If the preacher stands and looks in one area of the congregation for a long time, the people start to get nervous. They say, "What's he going to know about me? What's God telling him?" But you don't know *everything*; you only know what God tells you.

The Problem With Flakes

When you get around some super-spiritual flakes, they act like they know everything. They'll look at you, nod their heads, and mutter, "Uh-huh!" And you want to look at them and mutter right back, "Uh-huh-huh!"

In a sense, the revelation gifts have gotten a bad name because of super-spiritual flake Christians who claim God told them this and that. God never told them anything.

Then you get the ones who are spooky, always seeing something spiritual. Everything that happens in life, to them, is *spiritual*.

My wife, Adonica, and I joined a lot of other preachers at a prayer meeting one night. Some people came up, took my wife's hands, and started prophesying about the great burden and oppression she was experiencing. She didn't know what they were talking about! She said she almost started crying for them.

Know that the revelation gifts are not natural revelation gifts. In the natural you can look at a fellow who's got holes in his shoes and holes in the seat of his pants, and you can tell that he's poor. He's so poor, he can't even pay attention!

So it's not such a great "revelation" when you call the man out and say, "Thus saith the Lord, thou hast nothing." And it's not a great "revelation" when the guy has a big cast on his arm and you say, "Thus saith the Lord, thy arm is broken." That's simply natural perception.

If you know people, you can pick up many things just by looking at them, being friendly to them, and spending time with them. You can know if they're happy or not. So don't come and say, "God told me." God never told you! When God *did* tell you is when you looked at someone and it was the total opposite of what you thought!

Speaking by Faith

I was in a meeting in Tennessee, minding my own business, when the voice of the Lord came to me and said, "That lady over there—call her out right now." She was standing by herself.

He said, "I'm going to give her a miracle: the thing that she's desired."

As I began to prophesy, I knew she was going to have a baby, but she was standing by herself—and when I looked at her hands, she wasn't wearing a ring!

I thought, *O God, I have blown it!*

But I said to the woman, "Sister, that which you have desired, and that which is impossible in the natural shall come to pass. God will give you a miracle. You've been desiring to have...a...a *baby!*" Eventually I said it. I thought to myself, *Look, I'm in so deep now, I might as well jump in all the way.*

She burst out crying. She was married; she just hadn't put her rings on that day. And she and her husband desperately wanted to have a child.

A year later I went back by their church and I held that baby in my arms. It came to pass, as God said. But in the natural, I thought I'd blown it.

Knowledge From Heaven

When it's God, you know. It's a *greater* knowing than head knowledge. It's a knowing down deep in your "knower." It's not that you *hope* so; it's "thus saith the Lord."

It's exciting because it's not your knowledge. It comes from Heaven above. It's imparted to you at a specific time, at a specific place, for a specific purpose. It will come, you'll know it, you'll share it, and you'll go on your way. It's not complicated at all.

Chapter 11

The Word of Knowledge

The supernatural gift of the word of knowledge is "a divine revelation from God that tells or shows us what is happening right now, or what has happened."

So the word of knowledge has to do with facts in the mind of God pertaining to the *present* and the *past*.

God will show you things in people's lives—not to put them down, not to discourage them, not to break them down—but to *help* them.

> God will show you things in people's lives—not to put them down, not to discourage them, not to break them down—but to help them.

If the gifts are ever used for anything but helping people, you will lose the anointing of God, and you will open yourself up for *familiar spirits* to dominate your life. You will begin to know things about people—but you will not know these things by the Holy Spirit!

I could give you many Scriptures on the subject, or point you to books written on the gifts, but I want to give you some practical applications to help you in your personal life.

God Speaks to Children, Too

The revelation gifts began to manifest in my life when I was about 12 years of age. One day I got home from school and went out and sat on the front veranda, just watching the cars go by. No one was home, and that was strange, because my mother should have been there.

As I was sitting there, I heard a voice. To me, it seemed to be an *audible* voice, but I'm not sure you would have heard it had you been there.

Do you remember the story of little Samuel? (See First Samuel 3:1-10.) He heard God calling him in the middle of the night, but the voice was not audible to Eli, the prophet of God.

When Samuel heard God calling him, he didn't know it was God. He thought it was the old prophet, so he ran to him, asking, "Did you call me?"

Eli answered, "No, I didn't call you. Go back, lie down, and go to sleep."

Samuel did as he was told. Then he heard it again: "Samuel, Samuel!"

Again he ran to Eli and said, "You called me."

"No, I didn't," the old man said.

After it happened a third time, Eli realized what was happening and told the child, "It's God speaking to you. Go back, lie down, and say, 'Yes, Lord, Your servant is listening.'"

The voice of God was audible to Samuel, but not to the prophet of God! So you could have been right there with me on that veranda and not heard what I heard. It was so loud to me, it seemed like someone was speaking over a loud speaker—yet it was on the inside of me.

However it comes, when the voice of the Lord comes, it is so loud, you can't argue with it. You don't say, "I wonder if that was God?"

When Saul fell down on the road to Damascus, after hearing the voice ask, "Saul, Saul, why do you persecute Me?" he immediately responded, "Who art Thou, *Lord*?" Saul answered the question for himself by addressing the speaker as "Lord."

The Voice on the Veranda

The voice said these words to me—words I will never forget—"Your mom will not be home today. She's had a car wreck. But don't worry; she's all right. She's in the hospital."

I looked around to see if someone was hiding behind the wall on the veranda, but no one was there. Half an hour later my father walked in the door. It was strange to see him at 3:30 in the afternoon; he normally came home at six o'clock at night.

He said, "I want to tell you what happened to Mom."

I looked at him and said, "Dad, you don't have to tell me what happened to Mom. I already *know* what happened to Mom. She's had a car wreck. She's in the hospital. But don't worry; she's all right."

He said, "How did you know *that*?"

I replied, "A voice spoke to me when I was on the front veranda."

Why did God do that? He did it to begin to teach me something. And God was right: My mom did have a car wreck. The car rolled eight times, but she was able to climb out the side window with absolutely no injury. Isn't God wonderful?

What was it? It was a word of knowledge.

Words of knowledge come as you're minding your own business. It happens to me all the time in the congregation.

I'll be walking along, look across the congregation, and suddenly I'll see someone who stands out to me.

Then, I'll hear the Lord say something. It might be a phrase, a word, a sentence—things God wants them to know. I follow through with it. Usually, I'll wait for it to come two or three times for confirmation. I'll wait on the anointing.

The Smile of Conviction

I was pastoring in a certain city, and we had problems with one of the gentlemen in our church. He had just come to the Lord. One day I woke up praying, and the Lord said to me, "Brother So-and-so is drinking again."

I *knew* it. I didn't see any booze bottles. I didn't have to! God spoke to me about it. It confirmed what someone in the congregation had told me.

If you are a pastor, you hear a lot of things. When people say things among themselves, it has a way of getting back to the pastor via the grapevine. That's what pastors are there for: to get all the feedback!

I knew this brother was going to attend a big fair that was being held in a country town. I also knew I had to go there, so I jumped in my car. There must have been twenty-five thousand people there, walking around looking at the different exhibits.

I really didn't know where I was going. Then I saw a tent with "Bar" on it. Before I knew it, I was going through the swinging doors. I walked right up to the counter, and there he was!

I tapped him on the shoulder. When he turned around and looked fully in my face, all I did was smile. I didn't say one word. I smiled, turned around, and left.

The man said, "I'm coming now; I'm coming now!" He ran out of the place, returned home, and God touched him.

How did I know he was there? Not because someone told me, for I didn't know where he was. But I felt the Spirit of God leading me, and I walked right in there and tapped him on the shoulder. When he saw me, his eyes nearly popped out of his head! He couldn't believe it!

Why does God do these things? To help people.

The Persistent Dream

I had a friend in the ministry whose church had grown from about 35 people to four hundred in two years. It was phenomenal what God was doing in his life and ministry. We were rather close, and we used to talk each week on the phone.

I had a dream one night—but it was more than a dream—it was a *nightmare*! I saw this brother in the dream, and I knew that he was in adultery. I *knew* that he was in adultery.

I got on the phone and called a minister with whom I was fellowshipping. I said, "You're not going to believe it, but this is what happened."

He said, "Look, brother, you'd better go and confront this guy if God's told you that."

But you don't go to a pastor and confront him with the word, "You're in adultery," unless you know what you're doing. Otherwise, you might become the next person launched into space!

I prayed about it, but still I knew, deep down, that the dream was true. The dream came several times. I rebuked it. I said, "It's the devil." I bound the devil. I said, "No, he's not doing any of that."

And God said to me, "He *is*."

So I drove down to his city and phoned him. I said, "I've come to see you."

He said, "I don't want to see you."

Then I knew something was up.

I phoned him back about two and a half hours later. I said, "I'm coming to see you, whether you like it or not."

He said, "Well, you'd better come on over then."

After I arrived at his house, he started in with the small talk: "Praise God, hallelujah, glory to God, we're in the Promised Land. Hallelujah, we're the head and not the tail..." I waited for him to finish. He ran out of talk after ten minutes, and then he sat there and looked at me.

I said, "Who is she?"

When I said that, he went pale. His voice became shaky, and he said, "How did you know?"

I said, "God spoke to me."

He told me it was exactly as God had said. His affair had been going on for ten months. This man would not repent, however, and in the end he lost his church, his marriage, and everything.

When I left his town, I was concerned and disturbed about his attitude. I asked, "God, why did You tell me about his affair when I couldn't stop it?"

The Lord said, "Because there's coming a time when the same thing is going to happen to another friend of yours, and you'll stop it before it ever gets out of hand."

Another Nightmare

Not 18 months later, I was minding my own business, sleeping away—I didn't eat any pizza that night—and I had another nightmare. When it happens twice in a row, you know it's God.

God showed me the man. He even told me who the woman was. And I prayed, "God, I can't go to this person!"

The Lord said, "You'd better do it."

So I waited for the right time and I got him alone. I said, "Today you stand at the crossroads of your life, your marriage, and your ministry."

He looked at me and his face turned ashen and several other colors. He swallowed and said, "What are you talking about?"

I said, "You and this woman."

His voice got rather shaky. "How do you know?"

"God spoke to me in a dream," I said. "Now you repent!"

He said, "Well, nothing happened."

I said, "Then you'd better repent right now, break all ties with her, and get back to what God's called you to do."

Thank God, I was able to put a stop to it, and today he still has a ministry, he's still married to his wife, and things are going fine for him.

Why does God do that: to destroy people's lives and ministries? No, to help people. God is in the people-helping business. And if you don't want to help people, you'll never have the gifts of the Spirit.

How Not to Have the Gifts

If you're running around blabbermouthing all over town, God will never tell you anything! That's one reason why we don't see the revelation gifts. If God told the Church half the stuff that's going on, they'd spread it to the newspapers and shout it from the television screens and the rooftops!

Instead of praying for someone, instead of uplifting him, instead of encouraging him, instead of standing hand in hand and helping him, they'd broadcast his sin: "Do you know what Brother So-and-so is doing?"

The Bible says, "Brethren, if a man be overtaken in a fault, ye which are spiritual, restore such an one in the spirit of meekness; considering thyself, lest thou also be tempted" (Gal. 6:1).

We don't see that kind of restoration in the Body of Christ today. If someone misses the mark, they're chopped off and thrown out in the rubbish heap. There are so many people on the highway of life who are on the spiritual rubbish heap, and God is tired of it.

He will not anoint people who abuse and misuse the gifts of the Spirit. In these last days, God will raise up an army of men and women who will lay their lives on the altar, who will love to touch people's lives, and who will not even count what other people say about them.

This army will move in the power and the anointing of the Spirit of God, and they will see mighty supernatural manifestations of His power!

Supernatural Parenting

These people will be driving down the highway and will know things supernaturally about their children. My parents are like that. As I was a kid growing up, I couldn't escape what God told them about me.

They would pray every morning at five o'clock. If I even thought of doing something wrong, they knew it. My mother would come to me and say, "What are you up to?"

"I'm not up to anything."

"Oh, yes, you are!"

"Why are you saying that?"

"Dad and I were praying this morning."

And I'd say, "O God, You told them! And it's not funny!" I couldn't get anything past them.

You can't be around the anointing of God and lie, carry on, and live your own life. People who are sensitive to God are going to pick it up. That's why people who get into sin don't want to be around the anointing of God. They want to run away, because they know someone's going to pick it up.

People who run out of our meetings are not living a life for God. They're bound by religious devils or other things. They can't take the heat, because when the Word of God is preached without compromise, their seat gets hot, and they want to get out the door! It's not necessarily because of what I'm preaching; it's because God is pointing a finger of conviction at them.

The World or the Kingdom?

You can't live with one foot in the world and another foot in the Kingdom of God and be around the power and glory of God. It will kill you. It will drive you out. You'll either get in, get out, or get run over! You cannot stay in the presence of God and keep doing what you want to do.

God will show you things only if He can trust you with them. And God needs to trust a lot of people in this day. There are things God wants to show you pertaining to the nation you live in and events that are going to take place in your everyday life.

For example, suppose you're in a partnership, and you're dealing with the world. You'll know by the Spirit of God when someone is trying to rip you off. You'll have "inside information"!

Some of you have experienced these things, but you've ignored the gift. You thought the knowledge was coming from your mind. You need to learn to discern between what's of the mind and what's of the Spirit of God. Once you know the difference, you can go with your inner "knower" knowing.

THE GIFTS OF THE HOLY SPIRIT

Chapter 12

The Word of Wisdom

Now let's look at the word of wisdom. Unfortunately, there are people who try to equate *natural* wisdom with the *supernatural* gift of the word of wisdom.

They assume that if you live many years and have great natural wisdom, you have the gift of the word of wisdom. No! It's God's wisdom that He drops on the inside of you. It might only be a sentence, and it might only be for a few seconds, but already you're walking a step ahead of the devil!

The word of wisdom is "a divine revelation from God that tells or shows what is going to take place in the future." It's the future; it deals with things that are to come. We can *know* what is going to happen!

People say, "I'm uncertain about the future." If you hook up with the known will of God (the Word of God) and begin to seek the unknown will of God for your life, God will begin to impart it to you by the Spirit of God. You'll be able to see what's going to happen one year, two years, three years in the future.

Seeing With the Eye of the Spirit

Everything we are doing today in our life and ministry we saw ten years ago and more. Nothing that's happening now is any different from what I saw happening. I saw it with the eye of the Spirit. You can see your future, too. God will show you.

I was about 12 years old when I heard the voice of the Lord for the second time. I was sitting in an auditorium in one of the East Coast towns of my homeland, the Republic of South Africa. I was minding my own business, listening to an American evangelist by the name of David Nunn preach the gospel.

As he was preaching, this same voice that told me about my mother's car wreck said, "You will preach here someday." I made a mental note of it.

In August 1983, God said, "Go to the town of East London and hold a crusade."

We went, and we rented the biggest auditorium we could find. My philosophy is, if you're going to flop, flop *big*! Personally, I can't stand small flops. Don't flop with a whimper; try to go out with a shout!

No one in that town knew me. We advertised the meetings, and the first night, three hundred people were there. That's a whole heap of people as far as I'm concerned!

But as I walked out on the platform, the same voice spoke to me and said, "You see, I told you you'd preach here someday." It took me back to when I was sitting there at 12 years of age. God showed me that I was standing that day on the platform as an adult in divine appointment.

The crowd more than doubled by the third night. During the three-day meeting, 124 people got saved. I said, "Lord, this is wonderful! This is great!"

Why did God do it? I believe He did it to show us that He is directing our life and ministry, and we are on track.

How to Find a Spouse

In 1981, I was looking for a wife, because the Bible says, "Whoso findeth a wife findeth a good thing..." (Prov. 18:22). I wanted that good thing! I was seeking God earnestly, praying several hours a day for a wife.

I said, "God, You know I don't want to marry some dingbat. And I can't marry someone who doesn't want to go into the ministry. (I already knew then what we would have to go through.) I've got to have the right person. Now, Lord, I don't know who to choose."

There's a wide selection out there! Many young people are so spiritual about dating, they're waiting for an angel to come down and say, "You may go out with this girl tonight." They'll never get married that way. Ten years from now they'll still be waiting for that angel.

Some young ladies want a Mr. Universe, and they look like a scarecrow. And some young men want a Miss Universe, and they look like the back end of an automobile wreck.

Often, they're praying for a glamorous person to come along when the right person for them is staring them in the face all along. But because that one isn't *their* concept of what they think they should marry, they continue to hold onto their image of what they think marriage is—a yacht in the Hawaiian Islands—and they end up marrying someone unsuitable.

Two weeks later, there's no yacht. And ten years later, she's got curlers in her hair, and he wakes up in the middle of the night and thinks he left the TV set on and a horror movie is playing. That's if you don't do it God's way.

Resting in the Lord

So I was praying, "God, You know. I don't know! I could get married to this one and find out it's a total disaster. But You know. You know her name, her model, and her number. You know what I need, Lord. I'm your child, and I stand upon the Word of God."

I was determined to find that "good thing" the Scripture promises, so I was much in prayer. I didn't run around looking all over the place for my future wife; I waited, because I knew God would tell me.

And one day I walked into a Wednesday night Bible study. There were about three hundred people there. As I looked across the room, *there she stood in all her glory and splendor*!

As I looked at her, I heard the same voice again that I'd now become familiar with, and that voice said to me, "That's your wife."

I said, "Hallelujah! Glory to God! I receive it! Praise God!"

You say, "What did you do then?"

You have to be bold and go and possess the land, so I walked over to her, introduced myself, and took her out. The first night I took her out, I said, "I'm going to marry you."

Two months later we were engaged, and we got married five months after that.

People often come to me, look me over, look at my wife, and ask, "Where did *you* get a wife like that?"

I look at them and smile. I say, "I got mine from God. Where did you get yours?"

So you can know, even about your spouse. Those of you who are seeking a wife, start praying! Those of you who are seeking a husband, start praying! But don't walk up to someone and say, "God told me I'm going to marry you." Unless you heard like I heard, you're going to be in big trouble.

Called to Pioneer

We were driving through a little town one day when God called us to pioneer a work there. It was a one-horse town. The one horse had died a long time ago.

The Lord said to me, "You'll start a church here." I turned to my wife and said, "We'll start a church here." We did. We stayed there for about two and a half years.

The town had several hundred residents. The church grew from a handful to about 180 people in two years, attracted people from six different towns and communities. I started the church on my twenty-second birthday.

God will show you things. You will know, not wonder. God will show you things to come in every sense of direction. This will help you know the will of God, because when you have the supernatural words of wisdom and knowledge, you can know things pertaining to your life in the future.

Prophesying a New Beginning

For years, we had been wanting to go to the United States. For six years we talked America, America, America—morning, noon, and night. In December 1986, we were praying the New Year in. My wife was lying on the bed and I was pacing back and forth.

I looked at her and said, speaking by the gift of prophecy and the word of wisdom, "This year our ministry will turn 180 degrees." Then I said, "That can only mean one thing: We're going to the United States. Get your bags packed!" Within one year we were standing on the shores of the United States.

God will tell you. You'll know beforehand. You'll have *inside* information!

Once I was in the States holding revivals, I didn't want to return to South Africa. We were so busy preaching Sunday morning and Sunday night, through to Friday morning and Friday night, two meetings per day. On Saturday we got in the car, drove to the next town, and started all over again.

We lived this way week after week and month after month. It had become a way of life for our whole family. We enjoy seeing the wondrous things God is doing, and we didn't want to leave it all to return home. But God started speaking to us about it, so we knew beforehand that we were going back.

God said, "I'll give you a sign within the next seven days."

The next day I preached to several hundred people at a certain church. I was just there for that one day, Sunday. The pastor's hand was shaking when he handed me my check. He said, "I don't know where this came from, but this was the offering we took in today."

He received a love offering in each service, and he never begged; he just passed the plate. When I opened the check, it was for $7,500 for one Sunday!

The pastor said, "I don't know what this means."

A Sign From God

I said, "I do. It's a sign." Our airfares came to $6,700.

Two days later we received invitations to preach in South Africa. Isn't God wonderful? He lets you know what's going to happen *before* it happens. You shouldn't get arrogant about it; walk humbly before God, and let everything along the way be a confirmation to you.

One reason I believe God wants to show us things to come is so He can give us a way out of future disasters. By showing us certain things, God can keep us from making decisions that would affect our life adversely. As we begin to walk in the supernatural along these lines, our life will become an adventure, because we really know what's going to happen.

How to Hear the Voice of God

The revelation gifts will not work in your life if you're running around all the time feeding your mind and your heart with junk. And if you want to start hearing the voice of God, you'd better get yourself quiet.

I have found that the gifts of the Spirit begin to operate best when I have become still before God. Then I can shut out the voices of people around me and my own mind and concentrate on listening for the voice of God.

> I have found that the gifts of the Spirit begin to operate best when I have become still before God.

When I go to churches to minister, I don't want to know about the problems of the people. Sometimes pastors tell you three hours' worth of rubbish about all their people before you even get to preach. Then you get in the pulpit and have the problem of discerning between what God's telling you about the people and what the pastor's already told you about the people.

Now when I go to a church, I say, "I don't want to know *anything* about your people, because it will be a greater miracle when I call a fellow out and hit the nail right on the head! If you tell me all the junk, I can't be open to hear the voice of God. And if God does tell me something, I'm still remembering what you told me."

You won't step into great revelations overnight. This is a lifestyle: God will tell you things as you live and walk with Him. Wait on the anointing. Wait for God to show you things. He will show you more when He can trust you with it. Then, when you're faithful with that little bit, He will increase it to even more knowledge, and so on.

Chapter 13

The Discerning of Spirits

*T*he supernatural gift of discerning of spirits is a divine ability to see or discern in three areas:

1. When the Holy Spirit is moving
2. The presence of demons or angels
3. False doctrine, false prophets; looking into the hearts of men (lies)

But it's not only demons that you discern through this gift. Everyone thinks discerning of spirits is just demons, demons, demons—here a demon, there a demon, everywhere a demon—but it's not.

I was in a certain man's meeting for four nights. This guy was a flake supreme with cheese on it! He was advertised as Evangelist Dingaling, who had the gift of discerning of spirits and revealing the secrets of people's hearts.

He would sit on the platform and *stare* at the congregation during the preliminaries. How would you like it if a preacher came and stared at everyone? There was no smile on his face—he wouldn't worship—he just *stared* at everyone.

After the offering was taken and he got up to preach, there was a mass exodus. People *flew* out of that auditorium! I thought, *What's happening here?* The people were afraid. It wasn't of God.

He'd call people out, and what he said to some of them was correct. However, there was no anointing present, and I believe he was getting his information from a familiar spirit!

He called one couple out and said to the wife, "You have kidney problems."

She said, "No, I don't."

He said, "You don't know it, but your one kidney is about to give in, and I'm just telling you before it happens."

He called another couple out and said, "Your marriage is on the rocks." They were the happiest married couple in the church!

With "success" stories like these, Brother Dingaling was soon exposed for the flake he was.

There's No "Gift of Discernment"

Please note that the gift of discerning *of spirits* is not "the gift of discernment." The doom-and-gloom "prophets" are always saying, "I discern... I see..."

The gift of discerning of spirits is not reading someone's mind, and it's not "the gift of suspicion," either. You can look at someone and suspect all kinds of strange—and untrue— things about them.

Actually, the gift of discerning of spirits operates in three areas.

Firstly, it operates in the area of the Holy Spirit, enabling you to see or discern *when and how the Holy Spirit is moving*. You'll know it supernaturally.

— 106 —

People will say, "That's not God," but you'll say, "Yes, that *is* of God." You'll know. When they ask you how you know, you'll reply, "I know *by the Spirit of God* that it's God."

There is a greatest measure of all three revelation gifts when they are exercised by the fivefold ministry. For example, there's a greater demonstration or measure of the word of knowledge, the word of wisdom, and discerning of spirits in the prophet's office than in a layman's experience.

Not everyone has the word of knowledge, word of wisdom, or discerning of spirits to the degree a prophet has. Of course, a lot of people call themselves "prophets" these days, but they don't profit anyone. They only "profit" themselves!

Secondly, the gift of discerning of spirits operates in the area of demons, angels, or natural human spirits. When this gift is in manifestation, you will be able to see or discern when angels or demons are manifested.

You will also be able to see into the hearts of people. In an instant, you'll know exactly what's motivating them. There will be a check in your spirit if something is wrong.

However, don't mistake this with natural perception. Sometimes you don't like someone because he or she gets on your nerves! Or someone offended you, and now you don't like that person, so you say, with spiritual superiority, "I have *a check in my spirit* about that brother." You should have *a check in the bank* and give it to him!

You don't have a check about him; you just got upset in the natural. It had nothing to do with the Spirit of God checking you about the person; it's just a personality clash. Lots of people have a personality clash and say it's the Holy Spirit. They say, "God revealed such-and-such to me about him"—and God never told them any such thing.

Protection Against the False

*T*hirdly, the gift of discerning of spirits operates as *a warning against false doctrine, false prophets, and false prophecies.* I call it God's alarm system for the Church.

This gift produces a sense of security in the Church against false doctrine, because you will know through the gift when false doctrine is coming forth.

You will also know *supernaturally* through the gift when someone is lying to you; it won't be by natural knowledge.

And, through this gift, you will discern false prophets and false prophecies.

I went into one meeting and the preacher was preaching and thousands were eagerly swallowing every word. I heard a voice speaking on the inside of me, saying over and over again, "Familiar spirit, familiar spirit, familiar spirit, familiar spirit."

I said, "Thank You, God," and kept on worshiping God. It didn't bother me a bit. God will show you, God will tell you, when something is false.

In another meeting, a minister was praying for the sick, and he called three people out. As he was about to pray for them, they all fell out. I nudged my wife and said, "That wasn't the Holy Spirit who put those people on the floor. That wasn't God."

The Same Holy Spirit

*T*he moment I said it, the preacher told the three people to stand up. "That wasn't God," he said. "A foul spirit threw those people over." That preacher has the same Holy Spirit I have.

When he said that, the demons began to manifest. The people became stiff and fell out on the floor again, foaming at the mouth. And he cast the devils out of them.

A baby Christian just off the streets will not know these things by the Holy Spirit. These revelations will come to people who are spiritually perceptive—to those who know the voice of God.

We've seen examples of false tongues, false prophets, and lying being exposed, but there's a powerful example in the Book of Acts that you will want to continue to study for your edification. It's the story of Ananias and Sapphira, found in Acts 5.

But a certain man named Ananias, with Sapphira his wife, sold a possession, and kept back part of the price, his wife also being privy to it, and brought a certain part, and laid it at the apostles' feet. But Peter said, Ananias, why hath satan filled thine heart to lie to the Holy Ghost, and to keep back part of the price of the land? Whiles it remained, was it not thine own? and after it was sold, was it not in thine own power? why hast thou conceived this thing in thine heart? thou hast not lied unto men, but unto God. And Ananias hearing these words fell down, and gave up the ghost: and great fear came on all them that heard these things. And the young men arose, wound him up, and carried him out, and buried him. And it was about the space of three hours after, when his wife, not knowing what was done, came in. And Peter answered unto her, Tell me whether ye sold the land for so much? And she said, Yea, for so much. Then Peter said unto her, How is it that ye have agreed together to tempt the Spirit of the Lord? behold, the feet of them which have buried thy husband are at the door, and shall carry thee out. Then fell she down straightway at his feet, and yielded up the ghost: and the young men came in, and found her dead, and, carrying her forth, buried her by her husband (Acts 5:1-10).

Ananias and Sapphira stood at separate times before the apostle Peter, lied, and were both carried out dead. How did it happen? Some will say, "Well, that was a word of knowledge."

Examining Hearts

It actually falls within the category of discerning of spirits, because this couple lied to the Holy Spirit. Their hearts weren't right with God. The manifestation of the gift was deeper than a word of knowledge. Ananias fell dead first, and later Sapphira fell dead.

Another scriptural example is found in Acts 16, the story of the damsel possessed with a spirit of divination:

And it came to pass, as we went to prayer, a certain damsel possessed with a spirit of divination met us, which brought her masters much gain by soothsaying: the same followed Paul and us, and cried, saying, These men are the servants of the most high God, which show unto us the way of salvation. And this did she many days. But Paul, being grieved, turned and said to the spirit, I command thee in the name of Jesus Christ to come out of her. And he came out the same hour (Acts 16:16-18).

This damsel followed Paul and Silas around, crying, "These men are servants of the most high God, which show unto us the way of salvation."

I'll guarantee you there were people in that crowd who said, "Amen, sister, amen!"

The Bible says, "And this did she many days." But Paul didn't pick it up immediately; he didn't know it immediately. One day, however, the gift of discerning of spirits began to manifest, and he knew it was a familiar spirit that possessed her. He promptly rebuked it and cast it out of her.

A third example of this gift from the Book of Acts is the story of Simon the sorcerer.

But there was a certain man, called Simon, which beforetime in the same city used sorcery, and bewitched the people of Samaria, giving out that himself was some great one: to whom they all gave heed, from the least to the greatest, saying, This man is the great power of God. And to him they had regard, because that of long time he had bewitched them with sorceries. But when they believed Philip preaching the things concerning the kingdom of God, and the name of Jesus Christ, they were baptized, both men and women. Then Simon himself believed also: and when he was baptized, he continued with Philip, and wondered, beholding the miracles and signs which were done. Now when the apostles which were at Jerusalem heard that Samaria had received the word of God, they sent unto them Peter and John: who, when they were come down, prayed for them, that they might receive the Holy Ghost: (for as yet He was fallen upon none of them: only they were baptized in the name of the Lord Jesus.) Then laid they their hands on them, and they received the Holy Ghost. And when Simon saw that through laying on of the apostles' hands the Holy Ghost was given, he offered them money, saying, Give me also this power, that on whomsoever I lay hands, he may receive the Holy Ghost. But Peter said unto him, Thy money perish with thee, because thou hast thought that the gift of God may be purchased with money. Thou hast neither part nor lot in this matter: for thy heart is not right in

*the sight of God. Repent therefore of this thy wicked-
ness, and pray God, if perhaps the thought of thine
heart may be forgiven thee. For I perceive that thou
art in the gall of bitterness, and in the bond of iniq-
uity* (Acts 8:9-23).

Revelation Is Knowledge

*A*ll *of the revelation gifts reveal something: knowledge.*
The word of knowledge is *knowledge*. The word of wis-
dom is *knowledge*. The discerning of spirits is *knowledge*.
You *know* something through the operation of these gifts.

Sometimes the revelation gifts overlap. Often, the word
of knowledge will come into manifestation with the word of
wisdom, and both will be linked to discerning of spirits.
Sometimes the manifestation will be so blatant that you will
know exactly which gift is operating. But at other times you
won't be aware of what is happening.

Regardless of how the gifts manifest, the result is the
same: You perceive things supernaturally by the Spirit of
God pertaining to situations in people's lives.

The last truth we need to realize about the revelation
gifts is that they may come in many different forms. It will
be different with each person, because God works with individuals. Therefore, God may not talk to you the way He talks
to me. Each of us hears the voice of God in a different way.

If we were all the same, wouldn't it be terrible? So the
manifestation of these gifts comes in different forms,
because God takes our personality and temperament into
consideration. That's why we must allow the Spirit of God to
begin to use us as we are.

Prophetic Prayer

*O*ften, when I take people's hands and start praying for
them, I'm actually telling them things that are going

to happen in their life. I may begin by saying, "Father, we just thank You for this couple, and we thank You for..."

My prayer then runs for two or three minutes, and it tells the couple everything that's going to come to pass in their life. It doesn't *seem* like I am prophesying—it *seems* like I am simply praying—but it is prophetic prayer.

There are different ways to deliver prophecies. You don't always have to throw in a bunch of Elizabethan flourishes, such as, "For thou shalt verily...yea...henceforth..."

You can go up to a person and say in everyday English, "You know, I was standing back there, and God spoke to me and said, this, this, and this." And you can give this word of knowledge or word of wisdom quietly.

If God shows you something, pray, pray, pray. If it's a tragic situation people are involved in, pray for those people. Uplift them. Love them. Don't ever allow your mouth to be used to carry tales of things the devil is doing in the Body of Christ. Zip your lip!

Becoming a Vessel

For the revelation gifts to begin to operate in your life, you must get alone with God. You must become a vessel through which God's power can flow.

When you get quiet, you drain yourself of the things of the world, and you become sensitive to the anointing. You begin to learn the ways of the Spirit of God. You learn how to test the spirits. You learn to know when God is speaking and when it's not God. You learn to know when it's your mind and when it's your spirit.

> The measure we yield to the Spirit of God is the measure that He will flow through us in the revelation gifts.

At times it's wise to seek confirmation from others. Sometimes when I get a piece of knowledge from the revelation gifts, I check it out with my wife. I say, "Honey, this is what I feel..." Or I check it out with ministers and other friends.

These revelation gifts—the word of knowledge, the word of wisdom, and discerning of spirits—are available to *all* believers. We can operate in them. We will flow in them in differing degrees. The measure we yield to the Spirit of God is the measure that He will flow through us in the revelation gifts.

Part Five

Conclusion

Chapter 14

Profit or Loss

After studying the subject of the gifts of the Spirit for many years, I feel that we as the Church are just scratching the surface when it comes to the realms of God that are available to us. Over the years there have been men and women who have stepped into those realms momentarily, but I believe that in these last days an army of men and women will arise and walk in the power of the Book of Acts. This book is by no means comprehensive—it is just enough to whet your appetite and hunger for more of God.

These gifts are as He wills—but I believe that He wills more than we will. The eyes of the Lord run to and fro across the whole earth—He is looking for someone to whom He can show himself strong (see 2 Chron. 16:9). Will it be you? God is just waiting to move to touch a lost and dying world with the good news of Jesus Christ.

When it comes to the supernatural, some are afraid that they might open themselves up to the enemy and be led astray by a deceiving spirit. There are safeguards that each of us can follow when exercising the nine gifts of the Spirit:

1. The love of God must be our number one priority. The gifts are there to help people and meet their needs, not to exalt ministers. Remember, I must decrease and He must increase (see Jn. 3:30).

2. Jesus must be the center of your life at all times. If you want to be protected you must live a *holy* life—remember it is the *Holy* Spirit. You cannot operate in the gifts and practice sin. If you do, you will open yourself up to a familiar spirit and be led astray.

3. You must humble yourself at all times to the Lordship of Jesus Christ, the head of the Church.

4. Everything that you do must line up with the Word of God and be confirmed by the unction of the Spirit.

5. The gifts are to *profit* the Body—not to destroy and tear down.

6. Our hearts must be pure at all times, not allowing bitterness, unforgiveness, and pride to take root. We must protect our heart with all diligence for out of it flow the issues of life (see Prov. 4:23).

7. We must not force the gifts. We must get in His presence and the gifts will begin to flow. They will be like a tumbling river, their source being the river of life that will flow out of our bellies (see Jn. 7:37).

8. The gifts of the Spirit are never to be used to manipulate lives or situations or with a money motive behind them. Beware that you don't follow Simon the sorcerer (see Acts 8:9-20) or the seven sons of Sceva (see Acts 19:13-14).

9. Give all the glory to Jesus. When God uses you in a powerful way, *always* give *Him* the glory.

10. Develop sensitivity to the Holy Spirit's leading. Don't grieve Him by the things you say and do. Keep a gentle spirit. Avoid a critical spirit.

11. Remember that these gifts, when displayed, will always be a sign to the unbeliever. Always give an opportunity for the unsaved to accept Jesus as their Lord and Savior.

12. When there is a public display of the gifts, don't allow the false or the flesh to muddy the waters. Bring correction, discipline, instruction, and rebuke if necessary—so that the Body can feel secure and know that they are safe to drink at the waters. Make sure you know who is ministering to you— where they are from and how they live—before you allow them to come and minister.

It's *very important* not to go and learn about the gifts from those who don't believe in them. These gifts are not passed away—as some would teach. They were not just for the apostolic age—they are for now. Remember that all of the New Testament writers were tongue talkers and were full of the Holy Spirit. Don't be ashamed of the Holy Spirit, and He won't be ashamed of you.

In Luke 11:11 Jesus said, "If ye then, being evil, know how to give good gifts unto your children: how much more shall your heavenly Father give the Holy Spirit to them that ask Him?" During my walk with the Lord—since the age of five when I gave my life to Him and at the age of eight when I was filled with the Holy Spirit and received power and a heavenly language—all nine of the gifts have been in manifestation from time to time. I am determined to press in closer to Jesus than I have ever been and to be more yielded than I have ever been before.

PROFIT OR LOSS

So, dear friend, don't be afraid—covet the best gifts. Yield to the Holy Spirit and embark on the greatest adventure of your life as you learn to flow in the Holy Spirit!

POSTSCRIPT

If you have been blessed and challenged by this book, please write to us here at our Tampa office or email us at testimonies@revival.com

We would love to hear from you. If you were stirred up and challenged to change and allow God to do His work in you, we pray that God would use you in a wonderful way to touch a lost and dying world.

Write to:
Revival Ministries International
P.O. Box 292888
Tampa, FL 33687

You can also reach me at
www.revival.com/prayer/testimony.aspx

or

call 1(813) 971-9999.

For souls and another Great
Spiritual Awakening in America,
Dr. Rodney Howard-Browne

The River at Tampa Bay Church
Easter Sunday, April 2014

The River at Tampa Bay Church
The Main Event, May 2014

The River at Tampa Bay Church
The Main Event, May 2014

The River at Tampa Bay Church
The Main Event, September 2013

The River at Tampa Bay Church
The First River Fest, January 2013

The River at Tampa Bay Church
River Fest, February 2013

The River at Tampa Bay Church
River Fest, August 2013

The River at Tampa Bay Church
Thanksgiving Fest, November 2013

Revival Ministries International
Campmeeting Lakeland Summer 2013

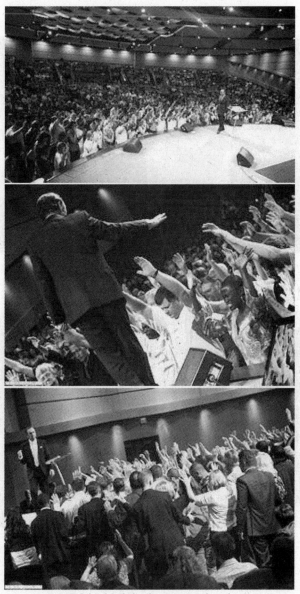

Revival Ministries International
Campmeeting Lakeland Summer 2013

The Great Awakening Live Broadcast
Night 200, July 2011

The Great Awakening Live Broadcast
Night 108, April 2011

Good News Umlazi
Umlazi, South Africa, 2005

Good News Soweto
Soweto, South Africa, 2004

The Early Years
Rodney and Adonica Howard-Browne

Rodney Howard-Browne
Singapore, 1995

The Howard-Browne Family
(Rodney, Adonica, Kirsten, Kelly & Kenneth)

About the Author

DRS. RODNEY AND ADONICA HOWARD-BROWNE are the founders of Revival Ministries International, the River at Tampa Bay Church, and River University in Tampa, Florida.

In December of 1987, Rodney, along with his wife, Adonica, and their three children, Kirsten, Kelly, and Kenneth, moved from their native land, South Africa, to the United States called by God as missionaries from Africa to America. The Lord had spoken through Rodney in a word of prophecy and declared, "As America has sown missionaries over the last two hundred years, I am going to raise up people from other nations to come to the United States of America. I am sending a mighty revival to America."

In April of 1989, the Lord sent a revival of signs and wonders and miracles that began in a church in Clifton Park, New York, that has continued until today, resulting in thousands of people being touched and changed as they encounter the presence of the living God. God is still moving today—saving, healing, delivering, restoring, and setting free!

Drs. Rodney and Adonica's second daughter, Kelly, was born with an incurable lung disease called cystic fibrosis. This demonic disease slowly destroyed her lungs. Early on Christmas morning 2002, at the age of eighteen, she ran out of lung capacity and breathed out her last breath. They placed her into the arms of her Lord and Savior and then vowed a vow. First, they vowed that the devil would pay for what he had done to their family. Secondly, they vowed to do everything in their power, with the help of the Lord, to win one hundred million souls to Jesus and to put $1 billion into world missions and the harvest of souls.

When Drs. Rodney and Adonica became naturalized citizens of the United States of America, in 2008 and 2004 respectively, they took the United States Oath of Allegiance, which declares, "I will support and defend the Constitution and laws of the United States of America against all enemies, foreign and domestic." They took this oath to heart. They love America, are praying for this country, and are trusting God to see another Great Awakening sweep across this land.

Believing for this Great Spiritual Awakening, Drs. Rodney and Adonica conducted Celebrate America DC, a soul winning event. They preached the Gospel of Jesus Christ for fifty nights in Washington, D.C., and surrounding areas from 2014 to 2019. Through the evangelism efforts on the streets, in the halls of Congress, and the nightly altar calls, 58,033 individuals made decisions for Jesus Christ.

During Celebrate America, in July of 2014, at the Daughters of the American Revolution Constitution Hall, Dr. Rodney executed a restraining order against the structure that is holding America in captivity, binding it and rendering it powerless and ineffective, from the Supreme Court, to the White House, to the Executive Branch, Congress, and the Senate, in the Name of Jesus. He commanded the Church in America to wake up and for the people of God to come out of their slumber. He declared that it is time to take the land.

During the Covid era, Drs. Rodney and Adonica took a stand for the Gospel of Jesus Christ. As a result, Dr. Rodney was wrongfully arrested at his home on March 30, 2020, for holding a church service at The River at Tampa Bay Church on Sunday, March 29.

As a result of his arrest, Florida Governor Ron DeSantis declared attendance at churches, synagogues, and houses of worship to be an essential activity. Dr. Rodney's arrest freed up every church in Florida to meet. All the charges were dropped by the Thirteenth Judicial Circuit State Attorney on May 15, 2020, and the date of his arrest and criminal record were expunged by Circuit Court Judge John N. Conrad on February 22, 2021.

Drs. Rodney and Adonica continue to take a stand for the Word of God and for billions around the world whose right to worship freely was removed and has not been, or perhaps will never be, restored. The Stand nightly services have continued for over 300 nights, as they stand for their brothers and sisters around the world who cannot stand freely.

With a passion for souls and a passion to revive and mobilize the Body of Christ, Drs. Rodney and Adonica have conducted revivals and soul winning efforts throughout eighty-five nations with the 300 City Tour, Good News campaigns, R.M.I. Revivals, the Great Awakening Tours, and The Stand. As a result, over 35,035,765 precious people have come to Christ, and tens of thousands of believers have been revived and mobilized to preach the Gospel of Jesus Christ. For more information, visit revival.com.

Connect

Please, visit revival.com or rodneyhowardbrowne.com for our latest updates and news. Many of our services are live online. Additionally, many of our recorded services are available on Video on Demand.

For a listing of Drs. Rodney and Adonica Howard-Browne's products and itinerary, please, visit revival.com. To download the soul-winning tools for free, please, visit revival.com and click on Soul-winning Tools.

- **Like us on Facebook:**
  Facebook.com/rodneyadonicahowardbrowne
- **Follow us on Twitter:** @rhowardbrowne
- **Follow us on YouTube:**
  YouTube.com/rodneyhowardbrowne
- **Follow us on Instagram:** @rodneyhowardbrowne

Other Books and Resources by Rodney Howard-Browne

BOOKS

The Phantom Virus
Socialism Under the Microscope
God's Top Ten
Perpetual Harvest
Killing the Planet: How a Financial Cartel Doomed Mankind
The Anointing
The Killing of Uncle of Sam: The Demise of the United States of America
Thoughts on Stewardship
The Coming Revival
This Present Glory
The Touch of God
The Gifts of the Holy Spirit
The Reality of Life After Death
Seeing Jesus as He Really Is
The Curse Is Not Greater than the Blessing
How to Increase and Release the Anointing
School of the Spirit
The Anointing
Manifesting the Holy Ghost
What Gifts Do You Bring the King?
Prayer Journal
Sowing in Famine

AUDIO CDS

Prayer Time

Weapons of Our Warfare

Becoming One Flesh

Faith

Flowing in the Holy Ghost

How to Flow in the Anointing

Igniting the Fire

In Search of the Anointing

Prayer that Moves Mountains

Accelerate

The Camels are Coming

Pray Without Ceasing Vol.1

Pray Without Ceasing Vol.2

The Touch of God

Mountain Moving Prayer

Having an Encounter with God

God's Mandate

The Anointing is Transferable

Dealing with Offenses

The Vow and the Decree

Whosoever Can Get Whatsoever

Run to the Water

Demonstrations of the Spirit and of Power

The Double Portion

More Than Laughter

The Hand of the Lord

Running the Heavenly Race

The Holy Spirit, His Purpose & Power

The Power to Create Wealth

Walking in Heaven's Light

All These Blessings
A Surplus of Prosperity
The Joy of the Lord is My Strength
Prayer Secrets
Communion–The Table of the Lord
My Roadmap
My Mission–My Purpose
My Heart
My Family
My Worship
Decreeing Faith
Ingredients of Revival
Fear Not
Matters of the Heart by Dr. Adonica Howard-Browne
My Treasure
My Absolutes
My Father
My Crowns
My Comforter & Helper
Renewing the Mind
Seated in High Places
Triumphant Entry
Merchandising and Trafficking the Anointing
My Prayer Life
My Jesus
Seeing Jesus as He Really Is
Exposing the World's System
Living in the Land of Visions & Dreams
Kingdom Business
Taking Cities in the Land of Giants
Spiritual Hunger
The Two Streams

MP3 CDS

The Phantom Virus

Socialism Under the Microscope

Killing the Planet: How a Financial Cartel Doomed Mankind

The Killing of Uncle of Sam: The Demise of the United States of America

The Touch of God: The Anointing

Knowing the Person of the Holy Spirit

The Love Walk

How to Hear the Voice of God

Matters of the Heart

Exposing the World's System

How to Be Led by the Holy Spirit

The Anointing

The Ways of the Wind

DVDS

Mountain Moving Prayer

How to Personally Lead Someone to Jesus

The Fire of God

Vision for America

Living the Christian Lifestyle

No Limits No Boundaries

The Curse is Not Greater Than the Blessing

God's Glory Manifested through Special Anointings

Good News New York

Jerusalem Ablaze

The Mercy of God by Dr. Adonica Howard-Browne

Are You a Performer or a Minister?

Revival at ORU Volume 1, 2 & 3

The Realms of God

Singapore Ablaze

The Coat My Father Gave Me
Have You Ever Wondered What Jesus Was Like?
There Is a Storm Coming (Recorded live from Good News New York)
Budapest, Hungary Ablaze
The Camels Are Coming
Power Evangelism
Taking Cities in the Land of Giants
Renewing the Mind
Triumphant Entry
Merchandising and Trafficking the Anointing
Doing Business with God
Accelerate

MUSIC
Nothing Is Impossible
By His Stripes
Run with Fire
The Sweet Presence of Jesus
Eternity with Kelly Howard-Browne
Live from the River
You're Such a Good God to Me
Howard-Browne Family Christmas
He Lives
Anointed—The Decade of the '80s
Live Summer Campmeeting '15
Live Summer Campmeeting '16
Haitian Praise
No Limits

The River at Tampa Bay Church

THE RIVER AT TAMPA BAY CHURCH was founded on December 1, 1996. At the close of 1996, the Lord planted within Pastors Rodney and Adonica's heart the vision and desire to start a church in Tampa. With a heart for the lost and to minister to those who had been touched by revival, they implemented that vision and began The River at Tampa Bay, with the motto, "Church with a Difference."

Over 575 people joined them for the first Sunday morning service on December 1, 1996. Over the years, the membership has grown and the facilities have changed, yet these three things have remained constant since the church's inception ... dynamic praise and worship, anointed preaching and teaching of the Word, and powerful demonstrations of the Holy Spirit and power. The Lord spoke to Pastor Rodney's heart to feed the people, touch the people, and love the people. With this in mind and heart, the goal of The River is:

To become a model revival church where people from all over the world can come and be touched by God. Once they have been not only touched, but changed, they are ready to be launched out into the harvest field with the anointing of God.

To have a church that is multi-racial, representing a cross section of society from rich to poor from all nations, bringing people to a place of maturity in their Christian walk.

To see the lost, the backslidden and the unsure come to a full assurance of their salvation.

To be a home base for Revival Ministries International and all of its arms. A base offering strength and support to the vision of RMI to see America shaken with the fires of revival, then to take that fire to the far-flung corners of the globe.

To break the mold of religious tradition and thinking.

To be totally dependent upon the Holy Spirit for His leading and guidance as we lead others deeper into the River of God.

Our motto: Church with a Difference.

For The River at Tampa Bay's service times and directions, please, visit revival.com or call (813) 971-9999. Location: The River at Tampa Bay Church, 3738 River International Dr., Tampa, FL 33610.

River University

RIVER UNIVERSITY is a place where men and women of all ages, backgrounds and experiences can gather together to study and experience the glory of God. River University is not a traditional Bible school. It is a Holy Ghost training center, birthed specifically for those whose strongest desire is to know Christ and to make Him known.

The vision for River University is plain: To train men and women in the spirit of revival for ministry in the 21st century. The school was birthed in 1997 with a desire to train up revivalists for the 21st century. It is a place where the Word of God and the Holy Spirit come together to produce life, birth ministries, and launch them out. River University is a place where ministries are sent to the far-flung corners of the globe to spread revival and to bring in a harvest of souls for the kingdom of God.

While preaching in many nations and regions of the world, Dr. Rodney Howard-Browne has observed that all the people of the earth have one thing in common: a desperate need for the genuine touch of God. From the interior of Alaska through the bush country of Africa, to the outback villages of Australia to the cities of North America, people are tired of religion and ritualistic worship. They are crying out for the reality of His presence. River University is dedicated to training believers how to live, minister, and flow in the anointing.

The Word will challenge those attending to find clarity in their calling, and be changed by the awesome presence of God. This is the hour of God's power, not just for the full-time minister, but for all of God's people who are hungry for more. Whether you are a housewife or an aspiring evangelist, River University will deepen your relationship and experience in the Lord, and provide you with a new perspective on how to reach others with God's life-changing power.

Programs Include:
- River Bible Institute
- River School of Worship
- River School of Government
- River Bible Español

You can be saturated in the Word and the Spirit of God at River University. Since 1997, River University has graduated over 4,000 students. It is the place where you will be empowered to reach your high calling and set your world on fire with revival. For more information about River University, please, visit revival.com or call (813) 899-0085 or (813) 971-9999.

God Wants to Use You to Bring in the Harvest of Souls!

THE GREAT COMMISSION, "Go ye into all the world and preach the Gospel to every creature," is for every believer to take personally. Every believer is to be an announcer of the Good News Gospel. When the Gospel is preached, people have an encounter with Jesus. Jesus is the only One Who can change the heart of a man, woman, child, and nation!

On the next page is a tool to assist you in sharing the Gospel with others. It is called, "The Gospel Soul-Winning Script." Please, make copies of it, fold it in the center lengthwise, and read it to people. As you read it to others, you will see many come to Christ, because as stated in Romans 1:16, *"For I am not ashamed of the gospel of Christ: for it is the power of God unto salvation to every one that believeth ..."*

Please, visit revival.com, click on Soul-Winning Tools, and review the many tools and videos that are freely available to help you bring in the harvest of souls. It is harvest time!

THE GOSPEL SOUL-WINNING —SCRIPT—

Has anyone ever told you that God loves you and that He has a wonderful plan for your life? I have a real quick, but important question to ask you. If you were to die this very second, do you know for sure, beyond a shadow of a doubt, that you would go to Heaven? [If "Yes"— Great, why would you say "Yes"? (If they respond with anything but "I have Jesus in my heart" or something similar to that, PROCEED WITH SCRIPT) or "No" or "I hope so" PROCEED WITH SCRIPT.]

Let me quickly share with you what the Holy Bible reads. It reads "for all have sinned and come short of the glory of God" and "for the wages of sin is death, but the gift of God is eternal life through Jesus Christ our Lord". The Bible also reads, "For whosoever shall call upon the name of the Lord shall be saved". And you're a "whosoever" right? Of course you are; all of us are.

continued on reverse side—

I'm going to say a quick prayer for you. Lord, bless (FILL IN NAME) and his/her family with long and healthy lives. Jesus, make Yourself real to him/her and do a quick work in his/her heart. If (FILL IN NAME) has not received Jesus Christ as his/her Lord and Savior, I pray he/she will do so now.

(FILL IN NAME), if you would like to receive the gift that God has for you today, say this after me with your heart and lips out loud. Dear Lord Jesus, come into my heart. Forgive me of my sin. Wash me and cleanse me. Set me free. Jesus, thank You that You died for me. I believe that You are risen from the dead and that You're coming back again for me. Fill me with the Holy Spirit. Give me a passion for the lost, a hunger for the things of God and a holy boldness to preach the gospel of Jesus Christ. I'm saved; I'm born again, I'm forgiven and I'm on my way to Heaven because I have Jesus in my heart.

As a minister of the gospel of Jesus Christ, I tell you today that all of your sins are forgiven. Always remember to run to God and not from God because He loves you and has a great plan for your life.

[Invite them to your church and get follow up info: name, address, & phone number.]

Revival Ministries International
P.O. Box 292888 • Tampa, FL 33687
(813) 971-9999 • www.revival.com